# *Slaughterhouse-Five*

## Reforming the Novel and the World

TWAYNE'S MASTERWORK STUDIES
ROBERT LECKER, GENERAL EDITOR

# *Slaughterhouse-Five*
## Reforming the Novel and the World

Jerome Klinkowitz

Twayne Publishers
Boston
*A Division of G.K. Hall & Co.*

*Slaughterhouse-Five*
Jerome Klinkowitz

Twayne's Masterworks Studies No. 37

Copyright 1990 by G.K. Hall & Co.
All rights reserved.
Published by Twayne Publishers
A Division of G.K. Hall & Co.
70 Lincoln Street
Boston, MA 02111

Copyediting supervised by Barbara Sutton
Book production by John Amburg

Typeset in 10/14 Sabon
by Compositors Corporation, Cedar Rapids, Iowa

Printed on permanent/durable acid-free paper
and bound in the United States of America

**Library of Congress Cataloging in Publication Data**
Klinkowitz, Jerome.
    Slaughterhouse-five: reforming the novel and the world / Jerome
Klinkowitz.
        p.   cm. — (Twayne's masterwork studies; no. 37)
    Bibliography: p.
    Includes index.
    ISBN 0-8057-9410-7 (alk. paper). — ISBN 0-8057-8126-9 (pbk.   :
alk. paper)
    1. Vonnegut, Kurt.  Slaughterhouse-five. I. Title. II. Series.
PS3572.O5S635   1990
813'.54—dc20                                          89-15280
                                                          CIP

# Contents

*Note on the References and Acknowledgments*
*Chronology: Kurt Vonnegut's Life and Works*

1. Historical Context      1
2. The Importance of the Work      6
3. Critical Reception      10

*A Reading*
4. The Monster at the End of This Book      21
5. What Do You Say about a Massacre?      44
6. The Reinvention of Form      66
7. History Transcended      86

*Notes*      107
*Bibliography*      111
*Index*      115
*About the Author*

# Note on the References
## and Acknowledgments

The edition of *Slaughterhouse-Five* used throughout this study is the first, published in 1969 by Delacorte Press / Seymour Lawrence (New York). This first edition has been reproduced photographically in all subsequent Delta paperback editions published by Dell since 1970. As a convenience to students who may be using the mass-market paperback of the novel that Dell has issued in scores of printings since 1971, and which has been reset, I have added its appropriate pagination after a slash.

The frontispiece photograph of Kurt Vonnegut was taken in 1966 by his student, Loree Rackstraw, at his University of Iowa faculty office where he was writing the first draft of *Slaughterhouse-Five*. I am grateful to Professor Rackstraw, now my colleague at the University of Northern Iowa, for permission to reproduce her photo, and for her many insights about Vonnegut's work. Jonathan Klinkowitz's extensive knowledge of science fiction was a valuable resource for locating Vonnegut's novel in relation to this subgenre.

Kurt Vonnegut himself has proven to be an amazingly tolerant and even amiable subject, despite having undergone, in his own words, the "therapeutic vivisection" scholars of contemporary literature are forced to perform. He supplied the two Vonnegut family letters cited in my concluding chapter, and has given permission to quote his fiction and commentary. He deserves my thanks for putting up with the sometimes unorthodox methodologies of current scholarship, as does my university, which in two decades of work on Vonnegut has been my sole source of support.

Kurt Vonnegut in 1966, in his faculty office at the University of Iowa Writers Workshop, where he was writing *Slaughterhouse-Five*.
*Photo courtesy of Loree Rackstraw.*

# Chronology: Kurt Vonnegut's Life and Works

1922        Born 11 November 1922 as the third and last child of Kurt
            Vonnegut, Sr., an architect, and Edith Lieber Vonnegut, daugh-
            ter of a socially prominent family of business and professional
            leaders, in Indianapolis, Indiana.

1929        Stock market crash and subsequent depression lowers the
            Vonneguts' standard of living; family moves from its elegant
            mansion to humbler quarters, and young Kurt is unable to at-
            tend the private schools his parents had chosen for his older
            brother and sister; however, he glories in the egalitarian atmo-
            sphere of the excellent Indianapolis public schools.

1936–1940   Attends Shortridge High School in Indianapolis, becoming
            Tuesday editor of its unique daily paper.

1940–1943   Attends Cornell University, Ithaca, New York, where his father
            (discouraged with the economic pitfalls of the arts) has encour-
            aged him to study "something useful"; majors in chemistry and
            biology in preparation for a career as a biochemist, but his high
            school newspaper experience helps earn him a job as managing
            editor and columnist for the students' independent daily, the
            *Cornell Sun*. Hospitalization for pneumonia during his junior
            year costs Vonnegut his draft deferment, and so he enlists in the
            United States Army.

1943–1944   Attends Carnegie Institute of Technology and the University of
            Tennessee as part of his military training, studying mechanical
            engineering. Before shipping out to England, returns home in
            May 1944, where on Mother's Day his mother commits suicide
            with an overdose of sleeping pills (throughout his career
            Vonnegut will remark upon the dangerous legacy of suicides:
            that they have left their children with that option themselves).
            Receives further training in artillery and as an advance infantry
            scout, and as the latter he joins the 106th Infantry Division

overseas, whose 2nd Battalion, 423rd Regiment, is almost at once decimated by the Wehrmacht's last major offensive, the Battle of the Bulge. Captured on 19 December 1944 and interned by the Germans as a prisoner of war and sent by rail to Dresden in southeastern Germany, where he is put to work in a factory. Because Dresden, an architectural and artistic treasure, has been declared an "open city," Vonnegut considers his war safely over.

1945        On the evening of 13–14 February, Dresden is destroyed in a controversial fire-storm raid by bombers of the Royal Air Force and the U.S. Army Air Force; German casualties are estimated at 135,000 to 250,000. Vonnegut and his platoon of workers survive because they are quartered in a meat locker far enough underground to escape asphyxiation and incineration. Pressed into service as a corpse miner, Vonnegut participates in the cleanup of the city. By late April the advancing Russian Army scares away Vonnegut's guards, and after a confusing interregnum following the German capitulation on 8 May Vonnegut is repatriated to the American forces on 22 May. Following rehabilitation in France and at home, he marries his childhood sweetheart, Jane Cox, on 1 September and moves to Chicago to begin graduate work in anthropology at the University of Chicago.

1946–1947   Studies anthropology (which influences his later fiction) and works part-time as a reporter for the City News Bureau. Leaves Chicago with his masters-level coursework completed but his thesis topic rejected (a comparative study of two "revolutionary groups": the American Plains Indians' Ghost Dance Society and the cubist painters, an approach at the time discouraged because of a presumed disjunction between primitive and civilized models). Moves to Schenectady, New York, and works as a publicist for the General Electric Corporation's Research Laboratory, where his brother Bernard is an eminent atmospheric physicist; enjoys the company of scientists whose training he has shared but becomes increasingly frustrated with the limitations of postwar corporate life.

1950        "Report on the Barnhouse Effect," his first published story, appears in *Collier's* magazine, 11 February; leaves General Electric and Schenectady to live in Massachusetts on Cape Cod and earn his living by writing fiction full time.

1952        *Player Piano*, his first novel, published by Charles Scribner's Sons; sells a succession of short stories, based on events of the day (such as the Korean War, military developments reaching the edge of space, and the common practices of American middle-class life) to popular family magazines such as *Collier's* and the *Saturday Evening Post.*

1953–1958    Sells more short stories, and supplements income by such odd jobs as writing public relations copy, running an imported automobile dealership, selling a piece of fabricated sculpture to the Airport Commission in Boston, and teaching at a school for emotionally disturbed children.

1958    On 15 September Vonnegut's brother-in-law dies in a railway accident and, a few days later, his wife, Kurt's sister Alice, dies of cancer; Kurt and his wife Jane adopt their three children, suddenly turning a household of five into an extended family of eight.

1959    Publishes second novel, *The Sirens of Titan,* as a paperback original with Dell; begins exploring this new mode of publishing as an alternative source of income as his short story markets begin to dry up.

1961    Publishes collection of short stories, *Canary in a Cat House,* as a paperback original with Fawcett.

1962    Publishes *Mother Night* as a paperback original with Fawcett.

1963    Publishes "Lovers Anonymous" in *Redbook* (October) as his last family magazine short story, and sees "The Hyannis Port Story" killed in galleys by the *Saturday Evening Post* after the assassination of President John F. Kennedy (a character in the story) on 22 November; *Cat's Cradle* published as a hardcover original with Holt, Rinehart & Winston.

1964    Begins publishing essays and reviews in *Venture—Traveler's World, Life,* the *New York Times Book Review,* and eventually *Esquire* and *Harper's,* commenting on the popular and political culture of the 1960s; his comically inventive review of *The Random House Dictionary* (*New York Times Book Review,* 30 October 1966, 1, 56) brings him to the attention of publisher Seymour Lawrence; *Cat's Cradle* reprinted as a Dell paperback, while *God Bless You, Mr. Rosewater* appears as a hardcover original with Holt, Rinehart & Winston, attracting serious review attention for Vonnegut for the first time since *Player Piano* in 1952.

1965–1967    Leaves Cape Cod to begin a two-year residency at the University of Iowa Writers Workshop; faculty colleagues include José Donoso, Nelson Algren, Richard Yates, and Robert Scholes. Paperback reissues of his novels fuel a growing underground reputation among the era's disaffected young people, while new hardcover editions of *Player Piano* and especially *Mother Night* (to which Vonnegut adds a revealing new introduction) attract serious critical attention, climaxing in the publication by Robert Scholes of *The Fabulators* (New York: Oxford University Press, 1967) featuring a full chapter on Vonnegut's fiction. Returns to Cape Cod.

1968     Guggenheim Fellowship gives him the opportunity to revisit Dresden. Publisher Seymour Lawrence, in collaboration with the Delacorte Press, issues Vonnegut's *Welcome to the Monkey House,* a collection reprinting all of the stories from *Canary in a Cat House* except "Hal Irwin's Magic Lamp" (*Cosmopolitan* 142 [June 1957], 92–95) and adding twelve other short stories, two essays, and a revealing preface by Vonnegut on his autobiographical and critical roots; Lawrence also signs Vonnegut to a contract for his next three novels, beginning an association that will last through the publication of *Galápagos* in 1985.

1969     Publication of *Slaughterhouse-Five* with Delacorte Press / Seymour Lawrence, which becomes a best-seller and establishes Vonnegut as a public spokesman for the age.

1970–1971     Leaves Cape Cod to live alone in New York City, where he participates in rehearsals for his Broadway play, *Happy Birthday, Wanda June*; serves as the Briggs-Copeland Lecturer at Harvard University; awarded an earned M.A. from the University of Chicago, which had rejected his theses in previous decades but now accepts *Cat's Cradle* as a valid contribution to the field of anthropology.

1972     *Between Time and Timbuktu* produced for public television and *Slaughterhouse-Five* released as a major motion picture. Covers the Republican party's National Convention for *Harper's*; elected vice president of the PEN/American Center; named a member of the National Institute of Arts and Letters.

1973     Publication of *Breakfast of Champions*; appointed Distinguished Professor of English Prose by the City University of New York, succeeding Anthony Burgess.

1974     Publication of the first volume of his collected essays, *Wampeters, Foma & Granfalloons.*

1975     Son Mark publishes *The Eden Express: A Personal Account of Schizophrenia* (Praeger).

1976     Publishes *Slapstick,* which is given a hostile reception by the New York literary establishment; with this novel he drops the "Jr." from his name.

1979     His first marriage having been dissolved after a long separation, he marries photographer Jill Krementz, with whom he has shared a household in New York for several years; publication of *Jailbird*.

1980    Publication of *Sun Moon Star,* a children's book written in collaboration with illustrator Ivan Chermayeff.

1981    Publication of *Palm Sunday: An Autobiographical Collage*, collecting his recent essays, addresses, and sermons.

1982    Publishes *Deadeye Dick;* his sermon *Fates Worse Than Death* is published as a pamphlet by the Bertrand Russell Peace Foundation in England.

1985    Publication of *Galápagos*.

1987    Publication of *Angels without Wings: A Courageous Family's Triumph over Tragedy* by Jane Vonnegut Yarmolinsky, his former wife who had died of cancer the previous December (an account of the adopting and raising of her sister-in-law's orphaned children); publication of *Bluebeard*.

1988    Performance of his *Requiem* by the Buffalo Symphony.

# 1

# Historical Context

If the major cultural and historical events of the American twentieth century did not exist, Kurt Vonnegut would have had to invent them in order to write the literature he has. Consider his birthdate: 11 November 1922, the anniversary of Armistice Day, celebrating the end of the world's most destructive war (historians remind us that even World War II, in which Vonnegut fought, produced fewer military casualties than the first). Consider his birthplace and the circumstances of his family: Indianapolis, Indiana, in the heart of the country's stable and conservative Midwest, where three generations of Vonneguts had established a large and secure extended family, central to the region's commerce and arts, and where young Kurt was expected to prosper in the center of a growing, even booming economic community. Consider the Wall Street crash of 1929 and the succeeding Great Depression, which robbed his family of its financial status, caused his parents to reexamine their values (demoralizing his father about the arts and pushing his elegant mother into a despondency climaxing in suicide), and forced Kurt into a more egalitarian life-style which he now credits as one of his greatest childhood treasures. Then high school and college as the 1930s ended and the 1940s began, studying "something useful" but being called into

1

the army to be of use to his country instead, resisting the German and Japanese challenge to the democratic ideals he had learned to cherish in the Indianapolis public schools.

Along the way there were books, of course—a well-stocked family library of the expected classics plus sentimental folk tales read to him as a child by one of the family's servants—but through his youth and adolescence there were also the programs produced during the golden age of radio comedy (featuring Jack Benny, Fred Allen, and Henry Morgan, plus many others), and the marvelous slapstick films of Laurel and Hardy— the actors to whom he would dedicate his novel *Slapstick* in thanks for getting him through the Great Depression and all of the other depressions, public and private, since. Thus Vonnegut's cultural education reflected the special nature of his upbringing: a mixture of high and low, with an emphasis on the redeeming features of the latter. Such a combination would provide the key to the manner of his literary craftsmanship, and an aid to understanding his American popularity and almost universal appeal.

But first, for both his life and for his work, there is the matter of Dresden. Kurt Vonnegut's combat service in World War II began in December 1944, when the 106th Division—in which he served as an advance infantry scout—assumed defensive positions for what would become the last major German land offensive of World War II, the Battle of the Bulge. Within days Vonnegut's outfit, the 2nd Battalion, 423rd Regiment, was overrun, and after wandering between lines the twenty-two-year-old private was taken prisoner by the Wehrmacht. Vonnegut was sent to Dresden, an architectural and cultural treasure of a city in southeastern Germany described in guide books as "the Paris of the Elbe." Assigned to work in a factory producing vitamin-enriched malt syrup for pregnant women, he might well have considered his war over, for Dresden was an "open city"—like Paris, an enclave that by mutual agreement would not be fortified or used for strategic purposes by the Axis and hence would not be considered a legitimate target for bombing by the Allies. Its population swelled with wounded veterans, orphaned children, and families who had fled from the Russian advance in the East, Dresden had for the most part escaped the bombing that, by early 1945, had devastated most other German cities. However, on the night of 13–14 February, the city was subjected to a controversial terror raid by British and American heavy bombers, creating an intentional firestorm of cyclonic winds that destroyed its central area and killed between 135,000 and 250,000 inhabitants, nearly all of whom were noncombatants (by comparison, the German bombings of England resulted in less than 60,000 civilian deaths for the entire war). Although Allied planners felt they could justify the raid, and despite the fact that within months the full extent of Nazi atrocities in concentration camps came to light, Kurt Vonnegut believed that he had been witness to a unique event in the history of warfare: the largest massacre in military history, outstripping even the atomic bombings of Hiroshima and Nagasaki to come later that summer. Because he was one of the few to survive the event, thanks to his work detail's quarters several stories underground in the meat locker of a slaughterhouse, he felt obliged to fulfill his survivor's duty and bear witness to the event he had experienced.

The postwar world, however, was not ready for such an act of witness. As political alignments shifted, with Germany and Japan becoming allies of the United States while the Soviet Union began to define itself in an adversarial role, the matter of Dresden was first classified as "top secret" and then, under embargo from the official air force histories being written during the Cold War, allowed to be forgotten. At the University of Chicago as a graduate student in anthropology, the repatriated young army vet and former prisoner of war found his professors unwilling to discuss any negative aspects of the war beyond Hitler's infamy and the Holocaust that had exterminated up to six million Jews and other presumed political enemies. And so Kurt Vonnegut found himself channeled back into the American middle-class style of life he had experienced before the war: completing course work for a master's degree as a student on the G. I. Bill, working for a large corporation (as a publicity specialist in General Electric's Research Laboratory), and eventually developing sufficient talent to support himself and his growing family by writing entertaining short stories for the family magazines of the 1950s—*Collier's, Redbook,* the *Saturday Evening Post,* and *Harper's Bazaar,* none of which was in the business of publishing soul-searching exposés of American wartime guilt.

The late 1940s and early- to mid-1950s were a boom period for the American economy, and not even the United Nations' "police action" in Korea from 1950 through 1953 could seriously disrupt the country's cheerfully materialistic mood. As the Roaring Twenties had both supported F. Scott Fitzgerald and motivated his short story narratives, so the American 1950s provided Kurt Vonnegut with a seemingly inexhaustible storehouse of materials for his stories and a ready market for their sale. But like Fitzgerald, Vonnegut was both inside his material (living a thoroughly middle-class life among other small businessmen and tradesmen, each supplying his or her product or expertise to the commercial interests of society) and outside of it (as a witness to fundamentally human questions about the meaning of life and death in the context of warfare, and as a trained anthropologist as well). Throughout the 1950s and early 1960s he wrote novels, none of them attracting serious critical attention or selling in any great numbers, but all of them experimenting with disturbing new subjects and innovative ways of writing about them. And as the magazines publishing family-oriented short fiction gradually went out of business, he began writing essays on the new aspects of American culture emerging in the 1960s, until in 1965 he could move for the first time into a world of intellectuals and artists—the University of Iowa Writers Workshop—and commit himself to writing the book about his experiences in Dresden.

If the American 1960s had not happened, Kurt Vonnegut would have had to devise them. Some critics feel that this socially, politically, and culturally disruptive decade invented him—and that like Fitzgerald in the 1920s, his popularity would fade as succeeding decades developed their own values and beliefs. That *Slaughterhouse-Five*'s disruptions of the traditional novel's form found a receptive audience in an America that had seen many other traditions and conventions threatened and in some cases destroyed or transformed is obvious, but assigning causality is a thankless task. Suffice it to say that Vonnegut's life and work have paralleled developments in American culture, high and low alike, for nearly two-thirds of a century. Since achieving international fame as a best-selling author with the publication of *Slaughterhouse-Five* in 1969, Vonnegut has sustained himself as a great public writer in the tradition of Mark Twain, addressing himself to major social, political, and philosophical issues even as he locates himself at the center of each succeeding fictional work. In recent years these addresses have taken shape as self-professed sermons, and he has even felt obliged to write and have performed a symphonic *Requiem,* replacing what he perceives as an unfriendly liturgy with a prayer more receptive to the humane aspects of death. Death, of course, is at the center of the Dresden experience; but so too is there life after witnessing all that organized, orchestrated killing, and coming to terms with both sides of this experience stands at the heart of Vonnegut's understanding of his and our contemporary American culture.

# 2

# The Importance of the Work

Death, as every artist knows, is the greatest test of a creative imagination, for it is the one personally unverifiable experience. Others die, and survivors comment on the event. But our own death is something we can only imagine until it happens. To that point, there can be no verification for the effective truth of what we have imagined; and after that point, there can be no reporting back. If one is a literary artist, imagining one's own death becomes the greatest challenge to one's creative art.

*Slaughterhouse-Five* is just such an imagining. In Kurt Vonnegut's life, its central subject is the one unspeakable event, the essential content that refuses to be structured in any traditional way because, by any conventional terms of measure, it simply is not there. It remains an unspoken presence at the center of his work, an experience beyond words in a novel that, by definition, has to be made of words in order to communicate its message and its feeling. Yet Vonnegut does indeed write a novel, creating a series of structures both generated by and surrounding the unspeakable act of Dresden's destruction—by his own Allied air forces, where according to the scientific and historical circumstances of the event he should have died himself. Yet Vonnegut lives: before the event and after it, squarely and self-consciously within the culture that enacted this unimaginable act of destruction. Not that he has a political axe to grind, for wars are eternal and death is surely universal. But from his own wartime experience he saw the need to speak about what everyone else was declaring to be beyond words (and in the process covering up with any number of traditional stereotypes, from machismo heroics in war movies to solemn profundities about other peoples' atrocities).

If the thematics of wartime death present a challenge, so do the formally aesthetic issues of writing any style of fiction in our era. Kurt Vonnegut was developing as a novelist just at the time when literary critics and theorists were declaring that the novel was dead. Social commentators would argue that the boundlessness of contemporary life and its unchecked potential for rude surprises—be they the atomic bombings in 1945, the commercialization of popular culture in the 1950s, or the rash of political assassinations and societal disruptions from 1963 through 1968—made it impossible for novelists to present in any fair sense an orderly appraisal of reality. Life and what we now knew about it were simply too large, while the fiction writer's arena, circumscribed by the limits of mere hundreds of pages, was too small. Theorists would add that the novel's traditional function of describing the world was itself an illicit activity, based as it is on the premise that words actually correspond to the items they are said to represent. Instead of a one-to-one identity between words and things, language was now seen as a self-contained system, describing not the world itself but merely a series of differences among linguistic signals. Therefore Kurt Vonnegut's frustration with trying to speak about Dresden was simply an extreme example of how any novelist in the postmodern world would find his or her attempts to deal with a universally recognizable content blocked by a supposedly unbridgeable chasm between word and thing.

Vonnegut's attempt to cross this gap sets the high stakes for the gamble *Slaughterhouse-Five* becomes, and his success in delivering a fully realized literary work is the measure of his book's importance. His experience with the matter of Dresden, coupled with the fate of the novel in his times, dictated that a traditional approach to the subject would not yield a suitable result. And yet because he had witnessed the largest massacre in modern history he felt obliged to bear witness to the event, and because he was a fiction writer by trade he had no choice but to use the novel for his form of expression. And so in the common American tradition of pragmatically working with what one has in a self-taught but personally responsible manner, he put himself to the task of writing *Slaughterhouse-Five.*

In the book itself, one sees virtually every familiar convention of the novel modified, overturned, or completely discarded. Its title page, for example, refuses to stop, modifying the title *Slaughterhouse-Five* with an addendum, *Or The Children's Crusade;* even that is not enough, and so a subtitle is added, "A Duty-Dance with Death." Vonnegut signs himself as author, but will not let his name stand alone. Instead, he fills the title page with a rambling account of who he is, where he has been, and what he is up to in writing this novel. As a result, the reader is engaged in the Dresden story before the novel per se even begins. Conventionally, one believes in the existence of an author, and has no choice but to believe that the book he or she holds in hand is physically real. The willing suspension of disbelief, which allows readers to accept the narrative action unfolding within the story, does not begin until the title page is turned, acknowledgments and dedications are noted, and the tale begins with chapter 1. But the first chapter of *Slaughterhouse-Five* flouts another convention by giving us not a made-up character in a hypothetical set of experiences but instead Kurt Vonnegut himself, the man so carefully described on the title page, who tells us that "All this happened, more or less" (1/1). Not until chapter 2 does the narrative about Billy Pilgrim's adventures before, during, and after the war begin. From chapters 2 through 9 these adventures continue, but not in chronological order; events from the 1920s, 1930s, 1940s, 1950s, and 1960s are intermixed, with Billy himself physically transported back and forth in time to experience the full range of his life in one continual present. Even then, the novel is not complete, for there remains a chapter 10 in which the author himself comes forward to tell how he is, with these pages, concluding his narrative—and advising the reader of what has just happened in the contemporary American life we share (the historical occasion is the assassination of presidential candidate Robert Kennedy on 4 June 1968, an event for which most Americans can remember where they were and what they were doing when they heard about it, just as Kurt Vonnegut receives the news as he concludes the writing of this novel). Hence the work of fiction Vonnegut provides remains as physically present as the flesh-and-blood person writing it and the equally real person reading it, an accomplishment traditional fiction (with its conventions of illusion) would disallow. Yet these same conventions had painted fiction into a conceptual corner; by playing with the arbitrariness of their convention-ality, Vonnegut paints his way out and delivers the literary text the world had said it was impossible to write.

# 3

# Critical Reception

That *Slaughterhouse-Five* was destined to be a masterwork is clear from its author's intentions, boldly yet self-effacingly stated in the novel's first chapter. "I would hate to tell you what this lousy little book cost me in money and anxiety and time," Kurt Vonnegut says on its second page, adding that when he returned home from the war he felt it would be easy to write about how Dresden had been destroyed, "since all I would have to do would be to report what I had seen. And I thought, too, that it would be a masterpiece or at least make me a lot of money, since the subject was so big" (2/2). Of course it was not that easy. Vonnegut struggled through abortive careers as a graduate student of anthropology and as a research laboratory publicist before taking up his trade as a fiction writer, and even then there were scores of short stories and essays to write, plus five novels, before *Slaughterhouse-Five* could take shape, nearly a quarter century after its author's first intentions were expressed. Indeed, the efforts to write this book constitute the form of its initial chapter, becoming in effect the first critical commentary on the succeeding parts of the novel. Here the reader learns how Vonnegut's Dresden story resisted the traditional format of war novels and even conventional narrative plotting, and how it turns out in the end to be "so short and jumbled and jangled . . . because there is nothing intelligent to say about a massacre" (17/19).

And so when *Slaughterhouse-Five* was published on 31 March 1969, the volume's first reviewers were prepared for what was to come. Vonnegut's own reputation had in recent years begun to grow, as colleagues at the University of Iowa discovered his long neglected earlier work and published critical commentaries, placing his career in a perspective some readers found attractive. The gently barbed irony of *Player Piano*, *The Sirens of Titan*, and *Cat's Cradle* intrigued C. D. B. Bryan, who could praise the themes of guilt and social responsibility engaged by *Mother Night* and *God Bless You, Mr. Rosewater* respectively, but who also complained about what he saw as Vonnegut's refusal to take things seriously, a flaw that made the author fall short of being a major satirist—a complaint that critics of Vonnegut's new novel would sometimes echo.[1] Robert Scholes took a broader view, accepting Vonnegut's approach in *Cat's Cradle* as black humor, a form of rational comedy whose satire expresses a subtle faith in the humanizing power of laughter. As a novelist, Vonnegut created sufficient latitude within which to entertain, but as a moral spokesman he could demand that people be more thoughtful about the human condition and the world's threats to it, a theme of *Mother Night*.[2] Together, Bryan's and Scholes's retrospectives on Kurt Vonnegut's five-novel canon alerted intellectual and academic America to the author they had encountered during his two-year residency at the Writers Workshop, who with *Slaughterhouse-Five* would become, for the first time, a best-selling and widely reviewed figure.

Early reviews in the spring of 1969 expressed astonishment with *Slaughterhouse-Five*'s innovative form, but felt more secure that these surprises were coming not from a young radical but from something of an old horse of a writer whose inoffensive stories had graced such a venerable institution as the *Saturday Evening Post* and whose earlier novels were familiar if critically ignored fixtures on popular paperback racks. These first responses were eventually codified by Leslie Fiedler, the authority on American popular culture, who could use the success of *Slaughterhouse-Five* as an example of how the death of the novel that threatened literature in the 1960s was really only the death of the elitist art novel, and demonstrate how Vonnegut's mastery of low-brow, popular forms allowed him to tailor his fiction to formulas that are in fact genuine myths.[3]

Three contemporaneous reviews from distinguished commentators representing a cross section of ages and interests provide a fair characterization of the book's success. In the pages of *Saturday Review* Granville Hicks, an eminent critic with roots reaching back to the socially committed fiction of the 1930s, became the first of a long line of analysts to compare Vonnegut with Mark Twain and *Slaughterhouse-Five* with that classic author's volatile combination of humor and moral outrage in such novels as *Adventures of Huckleberry Finn* and *The Mysterious Stranger.* Hicks's first words reveal an obvious influence, for just a year earlier he had met Vonnegut at the University of Notre Dame's Literary Festival, where the man had delivered "as funny a lecture as I had ever listened to." Students at Notre Dame had known of Vonnegut only as a science fictionist "and had talked of him as such," but hearing his speech convinced them (and Hicks) that "what he really is is a sardonic humorist and satirist in the vein of Mark Twain and Jonathan Swift." Such tendencies were apparent in Vonnegut's earlier novels, but the presence of the living author on the stage at Notre Dame and within the opening pages of *Slaughterhouse-Five* made them clear: "Now we can see that his quarrel with contemporary society began with his experiences in World War II, about which he has at last managed to write a book." Hicks devotes nearly half of his review to Vonnegut's discussion of authorial strategies in chapter 1, and praises the writer for this honesty with his material and for the risk he takes (and wins) by not attempting to describe the bombing raid itself. Instead, Vonnegut "sneaks up from behind," allowing his satire to encompass a broad range of topics, from education, religion, and advertising to a distinctly Twainish diatribe against the curse of free will. "Like Mark Twain," Hicks concludes, "Vonnegut feels sadness as well as indignation when he looks at the damned human race," yet he does not allow his deep compassion to stifle the necessary outrage all humans must feel at the needless destruction caused by war. "Even though he is not to be identified with Billy Pilgrim," Hicks advises his readers, the real Kurt Vonnegut "lives and breathes in the book, and that is one reason why it is the best he has written."[4]

Robert Scholes, reviewing for the *New York Times Book Review*, was similarly moved. He too had known the writer, studying his work and conducting the first major critical interview with him in 1966.[5] For the *Times* Scholes emphasized how in *Slaughterhouse-Five* Vonnegut was looking back, not just at the destruction of Dresden but at his own twenty-year career as a writer. Having waited so long to look back, Vonnegut found himself identifying with Lot's wife, who was turned into a pillar of salt for her infraction. Therefore his own first chapter judged the novel as a failure, even though the author confesses that he had to love Lot's wife because her act was so human. At this point Scholes turns from *Slaughterhouse-Five* to the apocalyptic context of the American 1960s in which it was written, and makes a more considered judgment of its worth:

The connection between the Biblical act of God and the destruction of Dresden is not accidental. Vonnegut's book is subtitled "The Children's Crusade." The point is a simple one, but it should serve to illustrate just where the gap opens between the "silent generation" and the present group of childish crusaders who are so vocal in preparing for a Holy Revolution. The cruelest deeds are done in the best causes. It is as simple as that. The best writers of our time have been telling us with all their imaginative power that our problems are not in our institutions but in ourselves.

Violence is not only (as Stokley Carmichael put it) "as American as apple pie." It is as human as man. We like to hurt folks, and we especially like to hurt them in a good cause. We judge our pleasure by their pain. The thing that offends me equally in our recent secretary of state [Dean Rusk] and his most vicious critics [in the antiwar movement] is their unshakable certainty that they are right. A man *that* certain of his cause will readily send a bunch of kids off to rescue his Holy Land. His rectitude will justify any crimes. Revolution, war, crusades—these are all ways of justifying human cruelty.

It may seem as if I have drifted away from considering Vonnegut's book. But I haven't. This is what his book keeps whispering in its quietist voice: Be kind. Don't hurt. Death is coming for all of us anyway, and it is better to be Lot's wife looking back through salty eyes than the Diety that destroyed those cities of the plain in order to save them.[6]

Destroying something in order to save it is a conceptual value of the Vietnam war, and Scholes's response to that war and America's debate about it colors his interpretation of Vonnegut. That as a fictionist he was funny, compassionate, and wise served, in Scholes's view, to make him a necessary spokesman of the times—as someone who could contemplate the horror of current affairs, face this horror without disguising it, and yet provide readers sufficient comforts and strengths to make it bearable. Supporting this appraisal of Vonnegut's role was an accompanying interview and background story that highlighted his moral preachment in a previous novel, *Cat's Cradle,* which ends with the world being destroyed while the apocalypse's final casuality meets death by thumbing his nose at whatever order of divine providence may have been responsible for all that has happened.[7]

Reviewing *Slaughterhouse-Five* for the *New Republic,* J. Michael Crichton saw fit to spend the first third of his commentary reviewing the history of science fiction, the second third relating its current popularity to specific aspects of the counterculture (Robert Heinlein's appeal to those professing sexual promiscuity, J. G. Ballard's and Roger Zelazny's acceptance among those who experiment with drugs), and most of what remained summarizing Vonnegut's previous history as a writer of popular entertainments within the subgenres of science fiction and black humor. But Crichton's conclusion, focusing on the new novel, made crucially important points: that the "age of seriousness" in which we live discounts anything funny as being suspect; that Vonnegut had made a career of appealing to the less serious elements of our culture; and that he had done so in a style that was "effortless, naive, almost childlike." Such a style would seem easy to readers who had not tried to write so clearly and directly themselves, but that very ease made it possible for Vonnegut to articulate what few others would dare speak about:

> He writes about the most excruciatingly painful things. His novels have
> attacked our deepest fears of automation and the bomb, our deepest

14

political guilts, our fiercest hatreds and loves. Nobody else writes books on these subjects; they are inaccessible to normal novelistic approaches. But Vonnegut, armed with his schizophrenia, takes an absurd, distorted, wildly funny framework which is ultimately anaesthetic. In doing so, his science-fiction heritage is clear, but his purposes are very different: he is nearly always talking about the past, not the future. And as he proceeds, from his anaesthetic framework, to clean the shit off, we are able to cheer him on—at least for a while. But eventually we stop cheering, and stop laughing.

It is a classic sequence of reactions to any Vonnegut book. One begins smugly, enjoying the sharp wit of a compatriot as he carves up Common Foes. But the sharp wit does not stop, and sooner or later it is directed against the Wrong Targets. Finally it is directed against oneself. It is this switch in midstream, this change in affiliation, which is so disturbing. He becomes an offensive writer, because he will not choose sides, ascribing blame and penalty, identifying good guys and bad. . . .

The ultimate difficulty with Vonnegut is precisely this: that he refuses to say who is wrong. The simplest way out of such a predicament is to say that everybody is wrong but the author. Any number of writers have done it, with good success. But Vonnegut refuses. He ascribes no blame, sets no penalties. His commentary on the assassination of Robert Kennedy and Martin Luther King is the same as his comment on all other deaths: "So it goes," he says, and nothing more.[8]

Vonnegut's presumed quietism and his refusal to make ultimate choices set many critics against his work, which in turn prompted a defense of *Slaughterhouse-Five* by religious journals and commentators writing from a theological point of view. Writing in the Catholic weekly magazine *America*, science fiction expert Willis E. McNelly insisted that acknowledging science's role in the Dresden holocaust and using science fiction as a way of understanding it provided Vonnegut with a "modern mythology" capable of facing problems "we cannot otherwise face directly."[9] By displacing his readers' perspective to the physical distance and timeless present of the planet Tralfamadore, Vonnegut was enabling them to cope with these otherwise inexplicable matters. From this Tralfamadorian point of view, death is merely a "bad condition in that particular moment," a condition ameliorated by being able to consider all of one's better, happier times:

> And *so it goes*. The phrase becomes incantatory; these are the magic words that exorcise, enchant, stoicize. They are repeated by Vonnegut and echoed by Pilgrim to convince Earthlings of Tralfamadorian fourth-dimensional reality. The words become a fatalistic chant, a dogmatic utterance, to permit Vonnegut himself to endure. In creating Tralfamadore, Vonnegut is suggesting that cyclic time or the eternal present will enable himself and mankind to accept the unacceptable. The sin of Dresden is so great that it will require an eternity to expiate. But eternity is not available to all men—only to the Tralfamadorians and the Pilgrim soul of man, and Vonnegut has, out of his science-fiction heritage, created both. (McNelly, 126)

Yet it was obvious that *Slaughterhouse-Five* was not simply endorsing a religious view of eternity as a solution to mankind's problems, for within two years of its publication a campaign began, continuing throughout the 1970s and 1980s, to have the book removed from public libraries and banned from school curricula because of its critical attitude toward mainstream religious values. In "Vonnegut's Attack upon Christendom," Peter A. Scholl summarized the first of these complaints and confirmed that "The ridicule and repudiation of Christianity in particular and religions in general which foster belief in a father-god who is concerned with or active in history are part of a recurring pattern in Vonnegut's writing."[10] Bokononism, the religion invented for *Cat's Cradle,* was fatalistic and deterministic, and "This element of fatalism appears in a new guise in *Slaughterhouse-Five* . . ." whereby "Vonnegut introduces and comments upon the story he tells not as the first person 'engaged' author-narrator of *Cat's Cradle,* but simply as the author" (Scholl, 9). Disagreeing with McNelly, Scholl insists that the narrative position taken in the later novel remains more complex and ambivalent than the Tralfamadorian way out, for if their outer-space view were to prevail, "then writing an antiwar novel is completely absurd and pointless" (Scholl, 10). Instead, Vonnegut takes the occasion to rewrite parts of the Christian liturgy surrounding the person of Christ, including the lesson intended to be learned from the Crucifixion: not that the persecutors erred by tormenting and killing somebody with connections, but that they mistreated anyone at all and hence must answer for their sins. The result is in practice Christianity:

> Vonnegut does not believe in the divinity of Christ, yet he seems determined to assert many traditional Christian values. He cannot stand the theology of Christianity, but would have its ethics. His books propose that absurdity lies at the heart of the cosmos, and thus making any sort of moral statement is at least a little foolish. Still, paradoxically, he insists that man must be treated with kindness and respect, as though he were the center of the universe and possessed of an eternal soul. In other words, Vonnegut has lost the Faith, has repudiated Christianity, its creeds and assorted institutions, but he has retained all the ethical reflexes which sometimes embellish that religion, though they normally rest upon a theological foundation. (Scholl, 11)

Scholl's appraisal of Vonnegut helped guide criticism of *Slaughterhouse-Five* through the 1970s; although Josephine Hendin would lament Vonnegut's supposed nihilism and attribute it to the psychological disorder of his era,[11] and Thomas L. Hartshorne would claim his war novel surrenders its social duty to a deterministic and even helpless response,[12] others would follow Scholl's inclination to see a sensitive and humane (if not categorically humanistic) author reinventing his novel's form in order to accommodate the practice of decency in a world that had made such a response all but impossible. John Somer agreed that Vonnegut's mission was virtually a religious one, a dedicated act of witness to an event he felt the human race needed to understand in order to survive.[13] In my 1973 study I saw the author synthesizing the two streams of his career, comprising successfully formulaic stories for and about the American middle class and self-consciously experimental novels that reinvented subgeneric forms for boldly new postmodernistic purposes, in order to produce a socially responsive yet aesthetically independent work of art in *Slaughterhouse-Five*. My subsequent studies have considered the anthropological model of comparative descriptions of reality Vonnegut brought to the American literary tradition, and his identity within the post-modern turn toward self-apparency of form.[14]

Two decades after it was published, and nearly half a century after Kurt Vonnegut experienced World War II and vowed to become a writer so as to examine publicly his understanding of the war's meaning, *Slaughterhouse-Five* remains not only an item for debate, but serves as a litmus test for critics' attitudes toward the nature of our times and the appropriate literary response within them. Few traditionalists appreciate Vonnegut's effort: Alfred Kazin and Clinton S. Burhans, Jr., deplore what they see as the diminishing possibilities his fiction allows for the expression of socially pertinent themes, while John Gardner finds Vonnegut's talent debilitated by "inadequate will," a moral energy "forever flagging, his fight forever turning slapstick."[15] On the other hand, Vonnegut's work has proved to be a rallying point for those scholars contemporary literature who feel that *Slaughterhouse-Five* is part of a breakthrough to new, postmodernist standards of literary vocation, with Ihab Hassan crediting the novelist's "honest perception of his moment" as a motivation for creating a style "both lax and gnomic" yet a vision that acknowledges "the ironic barrier of the mind,"[16] and my allying Vonnegut's effort not with Kazin, Hartshorne, and Burhans's company of Ernest Hemingway (*A Farewell to Arms*) and Norman Mailer (*The Naked and the Dead*) but rather with Ronald Sukenick (*The Death of the Novel and Other Stories*), Raymond Federman (*Double or Nothing*), Donald Barthelme (*Snow White*), and Richard Brautigan (*Trout Fishing in America*), all of whom write fiction contradictory of traditional form and none of whose accomplishments are praised by critics committed to a conventionally modernist novel.[17] But whether pro or con, most readings of *Slaughterhouse-Five* credit it with being a significant literary work of its era; whether one praises or denigrates the accomplishments of that era is another question entirely.

# A Reading

# 4

# The Monster at the End of This Book

The most arresting fact about *Slaughterhouse-Five* is not that it deals with one of the most controversial bombing raids of World War II. Nor is it especially unusual to encounter the schizophrenic nature of time shifts that propel the reader back and forth among several distinct periods in the past, present, and future, or that part of the novel's action takes place in outer space. All of these themes and techniques had been used in one way or another by Vonnegut's precursors in narrative art, whether they be mainstream chroniclers of war such as Ernest Hemingway and Norman Mailer, modernist experimenters with the nature of time and space such as William Faulkner and John Dos Passos, or science fiction writers such as Robert Heinlein and John W. Campbell, Jr. What distinguishes Vonnegut's novel is that its real-life author is present within the text: as the narrative's central character in its first and last chapters, and as a person who appears three times within the action that evolves in chapters 2–9.

Vonnegut's act of placing himself squarely within his fictional work calls many assumptions into question. Although the history of the novel in England and America has been characterized by various forms of authorial intrusion, rarely had an author placed himself or herself in the ongoing stream of patently invented, illusory narrative while at the same time maintaining his or her own absolutely verifiable historical presence as a compositional element. This practice, in and of itself, throws an entirely new light on the otherwise traditional aspects of Vonnegut's novel, and presents his readers with an experience quite different from the process they might be expected to undergo reading *A Farewell to Arms, The Sound and the Fury,* or *Rocket Ship Galileo.*

Henry Fielding's omniscient narrator in *Joseph Andrews* talks candidly about his manipulations of plot, and Laurence Sterne puts his own personality and whimsical fantasies at the action's center in *Tristram Shandy,* but Vonnegut's role in *Slaughterhouse-Five* is different. Even though Fielding breaks the illusion that the reader is participating in real life, the pretense that the narrator is telling a true story is maintained. In a similar manner Sterne relies upon a readerly consensus that accepts his posturings as part of the same story, a consensus that participates in the willing suspension of disbelief that allows an author to present something the literary arts have always been presumed to have been presenting: an imitation of an action. *Slaughterhouse-Five,* however, begins and ends not with an imitation of life but with the real thing—the historical Kurt Vonnegut, who has survived the bombing of Dresden, summarizing how he spent twenty years trying to figure out how to write this book and finally finished it the day after Senator Robert Kennedy, another verifiable historical personage, died in the public spotlight. What the reader is asked to participate in is not just a series of recounted events, but an immediately present act of writing—an act cued to equally verifiable acts in their own lives, such as being able to recall (as most Americans living at the time could) where they were, and most likely even what they were doing, when they heard the news that Robert Kennedy had been assassinated. In the Western time zone of the United States, people were finishing dinner; in the Mountain and Central zones, they were concluding their evenings; and in the East, many people were asleep for the night, although some (myself included) were roused by phone calls from friends still awake who had heard the news. In the final chapter of *Slaughterhouse-Five* Kurt Vonnegut does more than just tell what he was doing when he heard the first report of Kennedy's death. True, he was writing *Slaughterhouse-Five;* but in this novel's closing pages we see that shared experience become part of the literary work itself—a work that step by step has involved the reader in its on-going action.

That such an invitation for involvement was so well received, placing *Slaughterhouse-Five* on the best-seller lists, sending its publishers back for seven additional hardcover printings and eventually scores of paperback printings, and elevating Vonnegut to a position of fame and public spokesmanship, is not merely coincidental with the times in which this novel appeared. By 1969 an entire generation had lived with the temporal, spatial, and physical alterations of television and other forms of highly technologized mass communications, transcontinental and transhemispheric airline travel, and the transformed political, economic, and moral situation of postwar American life. That something as basic as reading habits was changing can be considered by looking at a popular children's book of the times, *The Monster at the End of This Book, Starring Loveable, Furry Old Grover.*[18] Itself a spinoff of the popular television series "Sesame Street," this text's fictive structure is uncannily similar to that of *Slaughterhouse-Five,* presenting an acknowledged "historical figure" (the television character Grover) within a booklet that introduces familiar novelistic conventions only to transform them by making the real story turn out to be the reader's involvement with encountering that person in a narrative experience.

*The Monster at the End of This Book* begins in traditional enough fashion, its brightly illustrated cover announcing its title and picturing the presumed central character, the puppet Grover, waving hello to the reader (just as he would customarily greet viewers on the "Sesame Street" program). But the book's first page mixes tradition and innovation by having Grover, who has remained present in the illustration's format, express his dissatisfaction with the necessary reprise of title, credits, and copyright. "This is a very dull page," he complains, as he is pictured turning over the lower right-hand corner to see what follows. Pages 2 and 3, however, catch him in his tracks, as he suddenly realizes the preceding page said there would be a monster at the end of this book. He asks the reader to confirm that fact, and reacts with deep shock: "It did? Oh, I am so *scared* of Monsters!!!" The next two pages show Grover enlisting the reader's support: if he or she will not turn any more pages, "we will never get to the end of this book. And that is good, because there is a *Monster* at the end of this book. So please do not turn the page." A child, of course, can always be trusted to do just the opposite of what he or she is told, especially when the source of such a command has done it himself—we must remember that the story began with Grover impatiently flipping past the dull title page, anxious to see what happens next.

The next fourteen pages of *The Monster at the End of This Book* consist of page turnings, which are resisted by Grover in a crescendo of hysteria as he tries to tie down, board up, and even block access to the next page by cementing together a brick wall. But the reader can be trusted to complete that most readerly of acts, turning the page, and so every other set of opened pages finds the furry little puppet buried in the rubble of his demolished impediment, forlornly begging the reader not to go on, because he is "so *SCARED*" of monsters.

By the second to last set of opened pages, Grover is on his knees, begging that the end not come. "The next page is the *end* of this book, and there is a MONSTER at the end of this book," he pleads. "PLEASE do not turn the page. PLEASE PLEASE PLEASE." At this point the reader may question his or her own morality in the affair: is it right that Grover, a sympathetic and now pathetic creature, be subjected to such terror? But as the last set of pages are turned, as they must be for the reading act to continue to occur, we see that there is a happy ending in store for both narrator and reader. "Well, look at that!" Grover concludes. "This is the end of the book, and the only one here is . . . ME. I, lovable, furry old GROVER, am the Monster at the end of this book. And *you* were so SCARED!" On the right-hand side of this double page appears a patronizing, forgiving Grover, who gently but authoritatively informs the reader that "I *told* you and *told* you there was nothing to be afraid of." Does this mean that the narrative ends with the reader's rightful role as generator of the story's action unfairly supplanted? Not at all, because one last page—actually the volume's endpaper—remains. And here is Grover, drawn smaller than usual in a position of abject embarrassment, admitting the truth in extremely small type, literally sneaking out of the book that has shown him to be a very foolish narrator indeed.

## The Monster at the End of This Book

In *Slaughterhouse-Five* Kurt Vonnegut uses his own historical personage much like Grover. He tells the story not in an aesthetically distanced
narrative manner, but in a voice identified directly as his own, a bold viola-
tion of the understanding that the person speaking in a novel should not
be taken as the author himself or herself. And the story concerns Kurt
Vonnegut—not a summary of events in which he plays a part, but a living
record of the book taking shape as he struggles with its form, a struggle
shared by the reader and to some extent activated by the reader who is
characterized as the audience who needs to receive Vonnegut's story. Au-
diences have expectations, and much of the business of *Slaughterhouse-
Five* is devoted to thwarting those conventional expectations. To satisfy
those requirements in traditional form would destroy the integrity of
Vonnegut's act of witness. And so author and reader must work together
to get the story down on paper and to make their way through the 186
pages of this book. Like Grover's narrative, the real Kurt Vonnegut as subject of this experience and writer of this tale is at the center of the action as
the novel begins and as it ends. So too is the reader, not as the passive observer of these events but as a self-conscious participant in the act of putting this book together and forcing its completion. Grover is a bit
embarrassed at what he and his readers have produced, just as Kurt
Vonnegut feels obliged to apologize to his publisher for delivering a book
"so jumbled and jangled" (17/19) and so small, given the magnitude of the
catastrophe it describes. Yet Grover's narrative has been a successful action
in terms of portraying not some other described action but rather itself,
and by accomplishing this same task *Slaughterhouse-Five* justifies
Vonnegut's seemingly disproportionate commitment of "money and anxiety and time" (2/2).

The person who appears at the beginning of *Slaughterhouse-Five* is
the real Kurt Vonnegut. Autobiographical notes abound, and are easily
comparable to the typical reader's own life, for most of Vonnegut's experiences appear to be a familiar story from America's middle class: education, some odd jobs, an abortive career in one of the big postwar
corporations, and eventually a more rewarding profession surrounded by
the paraphernalia of family life. That all this followed his military service
in World War II is scarcely remarkable, since three million of Vonnegut's

countrymen and women had accompanied him into uniform. Surely every one of them could have a story to tell, but chapter 1—much like the beginning of the "Sesame Street" booklet—presents something other than a recounted story and something quite different from a routinely described character. The key point is that Vonnegut appears on the first page of his book in the process of writing it. And writing it has not been easy, as he proceeds to explain in a way that enlists the reader's cooperation in overcoming the obstacles both author and reader face in making their way through a war story.

Postwar America, Vonnegut understands, has been well stocked with war stories. Publishing another, twenty-four years after the event, would seem to be a redundant act. Moreover, the plentitude of such stories, both in print and on film, has formed a mold for such narratives—a mold Vonnegut at first thought he could exploit for his own benefit. But the presence of those texts resists his, for what he wants to say does not fit the form through which society is prepared to listen. And so instead of getting on with his story, as any conventional storyteller might be expected to do, Vonnegut proceeds to write about how difficult it is to write. Such a strategy can be a facile trick, for in the process of protesting his inability to write the author has in fact written something down. But Vonnegut's tactics are more complex in their effect, for as he runs through the series of difficulties he has encountered in the process of trying to write a conventional war novel, he produces a radically unconventional war novel—a process which not only takes place in the presence of the book's readers, but with their active participation in the affair.

The obstacles Kurt Vonnegut encounters are for the most part other texts. Because these are texts familiar to his readers, they are as much a part of their lives as of his, and so producing a new text titled *Slaughterhouse-Five* becomes a joint venture arousing common sympathies and common frustrations. The first text Vonnegut and his readers have to deal with is a postcard, that most common of written intrusions into the stream of daily life. The card comes from someone in real life, a citizen of present-day Dresden named Gerhard Müller, who Vonnegut and his friend have met just a year before the present time of writing while researching their experiences in East Germany. Their meeting has been a random coincidence, as Müller is the taxicab driver who happens to be the one who takes them around the city, pointing out the slaughter-house prison of twenty-three years before. He also has a story, whose elements of past, present, and future complement Vonnegut's projected tale: Müller was a prisoner of war held by the American forces for a time. But his experience has generated no singular moral truth, for he was repatriated, worked to rebuild a decent standard of life after the war, and now lives in "a pleasant little apartment." His daughter is "getting an excellent education"—an acceptable but unexceptional life, certainly not the makings of a thrilling war story. There is one major detail from this life, tucked in grammatically with all the others: "His mother was incinerated in the Dresden fire-storm." To which Vonnegut can add nothing except "So it goes" (1/1–2), the first of one hundred such statements in the novel, uttered each time something living dies as a reminder that death itself is one of life's most common events. Müller's postcard, which arrives in time for Christmas 1967, conveys a simple sentiment: " 'I wish you and your family also as to your friend Merry Christmas and a happy New Year and I hope that we'll meet again in a world of peace and freedom in the taxi cab if the accident will' " (2/2). Müller's English grammar is comically if good-heartedly fractured; his syntax runs everything together with its series of undiscriminating "and"s; his one qualifying phrase, "if the accident will," throws what might otherwise be perceived as a historical plan into the randomness of unorganized chaos. What the meeting and the subsequent postcard tell Vonnegut is that neither the events of 1944–45 or of 1967 by themselves will make a remarkable story or even a coherently organized narrative. If he or his readers want to have a useful and interesting text, they will have to search elsewhere.

Müller's text leads to other texts, none of them any more helpful to Vonnegut in getting his novel underway. There is a limerick that reminds him of his apparently impotent memory, and a little ditty of a song whose last line repeats its first, yielding an infinity of replays without getting anywhere. There is the advice of a professional in the business, filmmaker Harrison Starr, who warns him that writing an antiwar book is as futile as writing an antiglacier book, or as futile as resisting death. Yet successfully resisting death is what every living thing does every day except its last, and so there is no reason for *Slaughterhouse-Five* to end on page three. There-fore Vonnegut pushes these obstacles aside and takes his readers on a jour-ney the history of which he *can* remember in exquisite detail, and the action of which does add up to something conclusive: the trouble he went through trying to write *Slaughterhouse-Five*.

Vonnegut's two decades of struggle with the book are narrowed down to just a few key items: his attempts to structure the events of 1945; his graduate student days in 1946–47 at the University of Chicago (during which time he also worked as a news service reporter); his re-search on the Dresden raid conducted in the later 1940s when he was liv-ing in upstate New York and working for General Electric; the first reunion with his war buddy, Bernard V. O'Hare, in 1964; his teaching at the University of Iowa in the academic years of 1965–66 and 1966–67; his receipt of a three-book contract from publisher Seymour Lawrence, which Vonnegut elected to honor by making the first of these books his Dresden novel; his return to Dresden in 1967 with O'Hare, a trip fi-nanced by his Guggenheim Fellowship; and his judgment that the book he has now written is a failure. But as his first chapters review these events in roughly chronological order, other interests intrude, moving himself and his readers back and forth in time and space, with the con-cerns of one era impinging upon the interests of another, until the entire personal narrative begins to blur together into one continuous present in which the writer, in the living presence of the reader, draws on several eras of the past to present a novel that has not yet been written (and of course not yet read either).

Consider the involvement with O'Hare. Chapter 1 begins with him and Vonnegut meeting Gerhard Müller. Telling the reader about this event in 1967 prompts the author to go back to 1964, when he used the long-distance telephone to locate this friend he had not seen since 1945. This takes the narrative itself back to 1945, so that Vonnegut can talk about the Dresden story's historical outline, which leads to a summary of his postwar experiences in Chicago and upstate New York, until the chronology catches up to 1964 and the trip to meet O'Hare in Philadel-phia can be detailed. But between the 1964 meeting and the 1967 Dres-den trip comes the book contract from Seymour Lawrence, which prompts Vonnegut to comment upon the form his finished novel has taken as he delivers it to Lawrence, which in turn reminds Vonnegut that he should caution his then draft-age sons that they should not succumb to committing war crimes or profiting from work contributing to such atrocities. He then shifts the action back to the 1967 trip to Dresden and how, when fog closed down Logan International Airport and O'Hare's flight could not land to pick up Vonnegut and the other Boston passengers, the author winds up leaving a day late after a restless evening with still other texts pertinent to his experience of writing *Slaughterhouse-Five*. Although the business with his old war buddy provides the general framework for these events, they do not conform to the orderly progression of history. Instead, Vonnegut's frustrations with the writing of his novel and the implications of its eventual completion intrude at every turn, making the complications with O'Hare just an occasion for Vonnegut's own involvement with the text his readers now hold.

Finding the proper form for *Slaughterhouse-Five* occupies much of this first chapter. It is at times a frustrating search, because in addition to the task of fitting the unwieldy shapes of experience into the more limiting format of an artwork Vonnegut must also reconcile his own historical presence with the aesthetic dictates that would, according to the accepted rules, take him out of the picture. He faces this predicament with his professors at the University of Chicago who wish to efface his own story of the massacre at Dresden with more dreadful statistics from the Nazi concentration camps. He encounters it again a few years later, when his request to the U.S. Air Force for information about the Dresden raid is refused because the facts are still classified as top secret. "I read the letter out loud to my wife," Vonnegut complains, "and said, 'Secret? My God—from *whom?*'" (10/11). The enormity of the camps overwhelms the significance of his own witnessed atrocity, an event that threatens to be written out of history. Yet the forms available for such testimony turn out to be useless or counterproductive, even the structures Vonnegut has employed in his own chosen profession "As a trafficker in climaxes and thrills and characterizations and wonderful dialogue and suspense and confrontations" (4/5). The year 1968, after all, finds him a veteran of four dozen profitable sales to America's most popular short story

markets and the published author of five previous novels. But their for-
mulae, by themselves, are no more helpful than the competing tales he
hears in graduate school or the total silence provided by the Air Force.
He employs his narratological talents to draw time lines for his new novel's characters on a roll of wallpaper, using his daughter's crayons. But all
he can visualize is some of those lines disappearing into "a vertical band
of orange cross-hatching" (5/5) that represents the destruction of Dresden. Many lines are consumed within this glowing band, which for now
eludes the author's powers of articulation (that glowing band will finally
have its day in Vonnegut's subsequent novels *Breakfast of Champions*[19]
and *Bluebeard*,[20] where it becomes the ineluctable presence of living self-
awareness as depicted by an abstract expressionist color-field painter). A
few lines emerge from this blur, among them Vonnegut's own and that of
Bernard V. O'Hare's. And so the author uses another "line," that of the
long-distance telephone, to take himself out of the timeless vacuum his
artistic imagination has become. This renewed connection lets him follow a third "line," the highway route from Cape Cod to Philadelphia, in
order to visit O'Hare. But in his buddy's company Vonnegut finds not a
rejuvenation of his memory but only more competing texts and disorder-
ings of chronological time.

The visit to O'Hare's home serves as the most discomforting event
in all of chapter 1's struggles with form. Expecting an evening of hoary
old war stories swapped in pleasant surroundings by a pair of happy old
friends, Vonnegut instead encounters a relatively tight-lipped stranger
who cannot remember very much at all and an obviously hostile hostess
who sets up her husband and his unwelcome friend at an antiseptically
infertile kitchen table. Once again his anticipations are confounded, but
for a good purpose. As Mary O'Hare eventually explains to him, the
stage set of "two leather chairs near a fire in a paneled room, where two
old soldiers could drink and talk" (11/12–13) that Vonnegut had imagined would yield a style of narrative she finds thoroughly unacceptable.
Such cozy circumstances, she insists, encourage veterans to think better
of themselves—to fancy the roles they played in warfare as appropriate
acting vehicles for the likes of John Wayne and Frank Sinatra—when in
fact individuals such as Vonnegut and O'Hare were "just babies" (13/14).

Her anger with the future author of *Slaughterhouse-Five* is motivated by moral indignation: she feels that such distortions of truth in the service of self-glorification not only produce fraudulent books, but books that encourage others to fight wars that should not be fought and to wreak destruction no one should have to suffer. But Vonnegut's response is more than moral. He agrees that bad models may lead to bad behavior, but he also examines the artistic implications of her complaint. Perhaps there *is* something wrong with the artistic forms his culture has provided. Therefore his duty is not to tell his war stories as others before have told them, but to reinvent the form itself. With his promise made, he leaves Mary's home with a sense of mission equal to what he felt when leaving Dresden in 1945. Back then, his dedication was to content; now it is to structure and form.

The first structural elements Vonnegut finds himself compelled to reorder are time and space. In the midst of his struggles to write this book he pauses to talk about his family life, the stability of which has been thrown off-kilter by his trials with the words that will not come. He is a late night telephoner—that is how he has got back in touch with O'Hare over all this time and distance—and sometimes tries to call old girlfriends late at night after his wife has gone to bed. To make contact across the intervening years and the hundreds of miles between Massachusetts and Indiana is surely a technological transformation of reality, especially when it happens instantaneously. But when the long-distance operator fails to change his world, Vonnegut is forced to try another form of technology, transporting his attention to Boston or New York by listening to a radio talk show. He can also radically alter the form of human communication by talking to his dog. But eventually his body winds down and forces him to bed, where his wife stirs and asks what time it is. "She always has to know the time," the author complains. "Sometimes I don't know, and I say, 'Search *me*'" (7/7).

These shifts of time and place anticipate what will happen to the protagonist of chapters 2–9, Billy Pilgrim. But here they are happening not to a fabricated character (who for the purposes of readerly illusion might need to have his travels justified by a narrative device such as science fiction time travel) but to an actual living person, whose actions touch the reader directly because they are addressed to the making of this very book, certainly a real enough thing present in the reader's hand. The Vonnegut we meet in chapter 1 accomplishes his reorderings of time and space with the aid of that most obvious and familiar of stimuli, alcohol. It makes his breath smell like mustard gas and roses, a combination that drives his wife away but seems perfectly acceptable to his dog. It also allows him to live in a continual present, his interests wandering from place to place while he himself remains static, seemingly eternal in the timeless condition of late-night randomness he shares with long-distance operators, a canine friend, and distant conversations he can monitor but not join. While anarchic, this condition is by no means unusual. Its disorder prepares the reader for the way Billy Pilgrim's experiences will be presented. But at the same time Vonnegut is establishing a more subtle sense of order beneath the apparently random chaos of his late night maunderings. That order is determined by the strength of associations among his interests, a pattern of connections among past, present, and future details that makes them *somehow* hold together. At this point in the novel Vonnegut knows they relate, even though he cannot yet articulate how. But he does know why: because they have happened to *him*.

Within Kurt Vonnegut's experience, one event will trigger mention of another. Not simply because of memory—the author's ability to recall wartime events has proven to be an utter failure—but because of a subliminal relationship he cannot yet satisfactorily explain. This sense of things hanging together for no apparent purpose constitutes Vonnegut's next major reordering in chapter 1 of *Slaughterhouse-Five*: the notion of causality. Educated as a natural and then a social scientist, with military training as a mechanical engineer in between, Vonnegut's understanding of cause and effect would seem to be more than adequate. But such sequential explanations elude him when it comes to writing his war novel, for he can find no appropriate words to explain a massacre. There are no human sounds he can remember from that fateful morning after—just the chirping of birds who have, like Vonnegut himself, somehow survived. What the birds say means nothing, and to human ears sounds like an answerless question: *"Poo-tee-weet?"* (17/19). When the author tries to talk about his experience, his attempts are rudely rebuffed, leaving him helpless to utter much beyond an exasperated two-word sentence such as "I know" (9/10), which the frustrated witness can only repeat and repeat again. Many of the things that happen to him he can only judge by saying "And so on," a tag phrase used several times in this first chapter and which in his next novel, *Breakfast of Champions,* is identified as that work's structural principle. "And so on" is a denial of causal order, but it serves as a device to move the narrative action along, justifying by the most minimal of grammatical connections what happens next. By allowing things to proceed as they do, with one following another as "the accident will" (2/2), Vonnegut encourages the reader to reserve judgment on the course of events until enough of them have transpired that a pattern can hope to emerge. Such patterning is a key to Billy Pilgrim's adventures, but in chapter 1 the historical events are happening to Kurt Vonnegut, just as the event of reading them from page to page is being activated by the reader. In this manner the author and reader of *Slaughterhouse-Five* begin their work by sorting out things together.

The order of these associations at first appears totally random. Chapter 1's first episode concerns the 1967 trip back to Dresden, where Vonnegut and O'Hare meet Gerhard Müller and hear his story, an involvement that climaxes when Müller's postcard turns up the following Christmas. Müller's optimistic greetings prompt the second episode, Vonnegut's exploration of other infinitely circular texts which, like an antiglacier book, show promise of going absolutely nowhere. For this second episode the author has gone back to 1945 and, in the course of just a few hundred words, worked his way up to the present, during all of which time he has been doing one thing: "working on . . . a book about Dresden" (3/3). The third episode jumps back to 1964, but with a fully justified transition using these same words, "working on my famous Dresden book" (3/4); in the passage that follows Vonnegut explains his habits of late night long-distance telephoning and stinking himself up with alcohol, both of which are repeated in later episodes of chapter 1, even to the point of using identical phrases such as "mustard gas and roses" (4/4, 6/7). This first talk with O'Hare centers on the business of narrative climax, which leads to the fourth distinct episode: the author's attempt to outline his story's action on a roll of wallpaper. But even this self-consciously technical business cannot hold Vonnegut's interest for long, since the matter of structure turns back into the stuff of memory, as the author recalls the physical details from his own repatriation two months after the bombing. These memories, however, are almost immediately qualified by their relationship to the book Vonnegut is now writing, such as who was the original for the fictional character Paul Lazzaro. The episode ends with Vonnegut's war-story anecdote about an idiotic English prisoner who believes he has looted something of great value. The treasure turns out to be a preposterously tacky plaster model of the Eiffel Tower, but that fact does not dull the Englishman's excitement. "He *had* to show somebody what was in the bag" (6/6), Vonnegut admits, understanding that however pathetic is its substance and however confused is its structure, the man's story is begging to be told. That jumbled sense of excitement, that need to express one's own record of participation, is what generates the story—not any intrinsic worth to its theme or classical beauty to its form.

Looking back on the first four episodes of Vonnegut's story, we can see the same generative excitement. What holds the four together is the author's persistence in telling about his experiences and the reader's ability to see how they are all linked together—linked not by chronology or by geographical space, but by the singular presence of Kurt Vonnegut himself within them. In the Müller episode it is his interest in the circumstance of going back to Dresden and meeting a fellow prisoner of war, but from the opposite side, who has the same happenstance attitude toward existence: things happen, the particulars of which are determined by accident, not the least of which is the accident of their meeting. The second episode finds the author caught up in accidental circumstances himself, intending to do a book about the destruction of Dresden by simply reporting on what he had seen, but finding that his memory fails, a fact that sends him into a cycle of infinite repetitions much like the way his 1967 visit has reprised his 1944–45 experiences there. As for his 1964 phone call to Bernard O'Hare, the experience allows more details about the war to accrue (their Mutt and Jeff characteristics, the irony of their fellow prisoner Edgar Derby being executed for the theft of a teapot) without being forced into a predetermined shape. That is how O'Hare's and Vonnegut's faulty memories save them: although the author is by trade a reshaper of narrative forms, the past provides no easily moldable materials to merit a conventional approach. Even mapping out the action, as the author tries to do, yields nothing more than an inexplicable conflux of colored lines and traces, out of which emerges a crazy Englishman with a pathetically feeble trophy of his own great adventure in the raid. Müller, O'Hare, and Vonnegut have this in common: all three have experienced a major event in the reshaping of modern history, yet none of them can express it in a commonly usable form. Having thoroughly reviewed the past in these first four episodes, both author and reader understand that conventional means of storytelling yield nothing of interest about Dresden. Action, character, suspense, and even irony have failed the writer's purpose. Obviously something else will be tried, because the book itself exists. Considering what can be done after reviewing the past and inspecting present circumstance occupies Vonnegut and his readers for the balance of this first chapter.

What can be done is *to read*. That is what the chapter's readers have been doing in their dutiful sense of at least beginning to read *Slaughterhouse-Five* and seeing what its author has to offer. In these initial pages the readers have seen him tell all they need to know about his own past—both in the war and in the struggles of writing that have engaged him during the two subsequent decades. They have also seen him play with structures—once again, structures for his war book and structures for his life. All of these structures devolve upon specific texts: the unravelling wallpaper scroll for purported lines of action in the Dresden story, and the continuously recycling of the nonsense ditty, "My name is Yon Yonson / I work in Wisconsin" (2/3), that by its very form keeps returning to itself and popping up again as the theme song of Vonnegut's life. Readers of *Slaughterhouse-Five* can even read a newspaper story he wrote as a young, part-time reporter, and learn how he was told by his editor to telephone a bereaved widow, impersonate a police officer by giving her the facts of her husband's grisly, fatal accident, and write down her reaction. Even this episode fits the subliminally coherent structure of chapter 1, for the reader finds Vonnegut in two by now familiar postures: telephoning people and finding himself with nothing much to show for it

("She said about what you would expect her to say. There was a baby. And so on" [8/9]). Most important, the author has provided his readers with something to do. By reading, they are performing their appropriate act. And at least so far they are reading what Kurt Vonnegut has written.

But soon Vonnegut begins reading himself. After promising Mary O'Hare that he will not make *Slaughterhouse-Five* a promotion vehicle for the heroics of Frank Sinatra and John Wayne—and that he will in fact title it "The Children's Crusade"—he and Bernard O'Hare start rummaging through the family library. To find out about the real Children's Crusade they look it up in a book at hand, *Extraordinary Popular Delusions and the Madness of Crowds*. Its author "had a low opinion of *all* Crusades" (14/15), Vonnegut notes, and quotes an entire page from this volume regarding the especially revolting details of this particular crusade's exploitation, greed, and infamy. History thus tells a radically different story than does romance, and Vonnegut retires to bed with a new understanding that his and O'Hare's children's crusade was neither the first to happen nor the first to go wrong. Yet his reading does not stop here, for Mary has placed another text at his bedside: *Dresden, History, Stage and Gallery* by Mary Endell, a book published in 1908. Endell's work describes an architectural and artistic treasure Vonnegut saw destroyed a generation later, but that destruction is no longer the point of irony he first thought it was (when remarking on Edgar Derby's hapless fate for stealing a teapot amid such universal ruin). Endell now tells him about a previous siege of boundless devastation suffered in 1760, complete with details about museums and galleries afire, famous paintings destroyed, and the city's principal church tower completely immolated. The fact that Kurt Vonnegut has witnessed even greater destruction, yet remains at a loss for words, is complemented by Endell's transcription of Goethe's account of his own visit to the devastated city. As the most sensitively expressive stylist of his age, Goethe would certainly be expected to have deeply felt words for this event. And he does—but in German, a language neither Kurt Vonnegut nor most of his American readers can understand. Yet Vonnegut reproduces the Goethe passage in German, so that the report can at least be read, if not understood. Once again,

Vonnegut's readers are allowed the freedom to perform their most typical act, even if in absurdly minimal fashion.

Understanding an apparently illegible text is something Vonnegut and his readers achieve only as chapter 1 ends. It happens in a context now familiar: within the fractured time and displaced spatiality of an airline layover caused by a fogged-in airport. With clocks and his wristwatch out of synch, the author becomes a prisoner of what they say; and with his itinerary similarly out of control, he finds himself living in a spaceless vacuum, neither at home where he would prefer to be or in Germany where he is supposed to be. But he has not entered this disoriented state alone, for two books accompany him: Theodore Roethke's collection of poetry, *Words for the Wind,* and Erika Ostrovsky's *Céline and His Vision.* Just as Vonnegut's temporal and spatial wanderings throughout this first chapter have left his readers with nothing to hang on to but his words, so too does he find himself suspended beyond any conventional semblance of temporal and spatial order with nothing to ground his imagination except reading material. And so like his readers have done during the dozen and a half preceding pages, now Vonnegut fulfills his role by reading what is in front of him and participating in its atypical sense of order.

Roethke's words speak clearly and simply to him, with the clarity of a Sunday morning sermon (anticipating the sermons Vonnegut himself would begin delivering in the 1980s). One wakes to sleep, as the airport layover experience has just confirmed; the wisest thing to do in such circumstances is to take this waking slowly. Fate is thereby not something to fear, because only what is necessary to happen will happen, and what good does fear accomplish in the face of such determination? As for individual motivation and responsibility, the program is clear: "*I learn by going where I have to go*" (18/20). Artistically, Vonnegut is learning what the younger generation of innovative fiction writers (Ronald Sukenick, Richard Brautigan, Donald Barthelme, and Steve Katz among them) profess: that form is the footprints we leave behind us in the sand. Morally, the author appreciates how one cannot be held accountable for what one does not know, but that in learning by going where one *has* to go responsibility will be accrued in the same way things happen. Whatever grand plan the universe may imply, one learns how to handle it only by handling it. Just as *Slaughterhouse-Five*'s readers have learned about this novel's unusual format by going where they have to go—from page to page as Vonnegut's experiences in trying to write it accumulate—so does the author himself spend time with Roethke's stanza, reprinting it for his readers so they too can ponder its implications both for Vonnegut's life and for their own upcoming adventure in reading the novel's next nine chapters.

Then there is the analysis of Louis-Ferdinand Céline that Professor Ostrovsky provides. Much later Kurt Vonnegut would reveal that reading Céline's war novels convinced him that death was too common and predictable to lose one's self in grief every time it occurred, and that a motto on the order of "so it goes" would be a more appropriate reaction.

> I know when he began to influence me. I was well into my forties before I read him. A friend was startled that I didn't know anything about Céline, and he initiated me with *Journey to the End of the Night*, which flabbergasted me. I assigned it for a course in the novel which I was giving at the University of Iowa. When it was time for me to lecture for two hours about it, I found I had nothing to say.
>
> The book penetrated my bones, anyway, if not my mind. And I only now understand what I took from Céline and put into the novel I was writing at the time, which was called *Slaughterhouse-Five*. In that book, I felt the need to say this every time a character died: "So it goes." This exasperated many critics, and it seemed fancy and tiresome to me, too. But somehow it had to be said.
>
> It was a clumsy way of saying what Céline managed to imply so much more naturally in everything he wrote, in effect: "Death and suffering can't matter nearly as much as I think they do. Since they are so common, my taking them so seriously must mean that I am insane. I must try to be saner."[21]

At the moment, as the first chapter of *Slaughterhouse-Five* concludes, Vonnegut is more obviously influenced by Céline's vision of time, although the French author's moral position toward death will become obvious soon after chapter 2 gets under way. "Time obsessed him" (18/21), Vonnegut learns, and to share this understanding with his readers he reprints the paragraphs from *Death on the Installment Plan* where Céline admits the truth of death but then looks out his window at the scene of living people bustling about in the street and "screams on paper, *Make them stop . . . don't let them move anymore at all . . . There, make them freeze . . . once and for all! . . . So that they won't disappear anymore!*" (19/21). A prisoner of disordered time, Vonnegut is here reminded how the narrative artist can rearrange time to fit his or her purposes—to literally stop time itself from ticking away in its inexorable progression toward the death of everything that exists. These two attitudes—that death is inevitable within the course of time, but that the course of time itself can be arrested by art—form the polar extremes in Vonnegut's story, telling him what he must do but also showing him how to handle it as it happens.

Roethke's and Ostrovsky's books are the reading materials Vonnegut has taken with him into the timeless and spaceless interval between Cape Cod and Dresden, but there is a third text he finds along the way. It is a Gideon Bible, something almost every hotel or motel room in America provides. Looking through it "for tales of great destruction" (19/21), he locates the passage recounting the wrath visited upon the cities of Sodom and Gomorrah. But it is not God's devastation that Vonnegut pauses to reflect upon. The fate of Lot's wife is what interests the author, because her act of looking back is something he can love her for, "because it was so human" (19/22). For looking back, she was turned into a pillar of salt—so it goes. Now Vonnegut risks that same fate by looking back at his own past. He has come to terms with a seemingly untellable tale by branding it a failure—as it has to be, "because it was written by a pillar of salt" (19/22). But pillar of salt or not, he has survived both the event itself and its retelling. Lest the reader distrust Vonnegut's claims, he throws away the last restrictive narrative convention and reveals what the book's ending will be.

That ending, the interrogative chirping we've been told is the only sound after a massacre, does not come at the close of chapter 9, even though what he announces as the start of his Dresden book follows as the first words of chapter 2. It happens at the end of chapter 10, in which Vonnegut reappears as the writer working on this narrative as it unfolds.

This final chapter takes the reader on a bit of time travelling, from 1967 (when Vonnegut as writer was seen visiting Dresden) to June 1968, when the novel has just a few pages to go. In the meantime, nearly all of Billy Pilgrim's adventures have been recounted, leaving only his experiences as a corpse miner and as a suddenly former prisoner of war who wakes to find his prison door unlocked. But Vonnegut wants himself to be "in there" (186/214) too—not as another supernumerary soldier as he has been on the occasions recounted within chapters 2–9, but as someone the reader now recalls as the writer who struggled so hard to get things underway in chapter 1. And he wants his readers to be experiencing this last chapter with reference to their own reality—hence the time cues to events that have happened within the past year (Robert Kennedy died on 6 June 1968; *Slaughterhouse-Five* was published on 31 March 1969).

There is even one last piece of unfinished novel-writing business to take care of. Nine chapters earlier, one of the first plot techniques Vonnegut discussed with Bernard O'Hare (and by implication with his readers as well) was structuring his novel's climax around the execution of Edgar Derby for stealing a teapot. Now, with less than a page before his book ends, the author must take what he first intended to be an instance of high climactic irony and toss it in almost matter-of-factly: "Somewhere in there the poor old high school teacher, Edgar Derby, was caught with a teapot he had taken from the catacombs. He was arrested for plundering. He was tried and shot. / So it goes" (186/214). In the context of this full novel, now ending, Derby's death is just one among hundreds of thousands, and the author's appraisal of "So it goes" counts as the one-hundredth time he has had to say it according to its formulaic repetition every time a living thing dies. Time itself has been reordered, for most of the Dresden casualties have happened after Derby's death. But Derby's is the last Kurt Vonnegut mentions, and by mentioning it in the process of this century number of "so it goes"s rounds out both the artistic form and moral context of *Slaughterhouse-Five*. Derby's death is ironic, but for a much greater reason than the petty nature of his crime. It climaxes the portrayal of a major holocaust. But its survivors have the ability to move on with their lives to the extent that time itself becomes a trackless jumble and the death of an intimate friend—surely the nicest person in the whole story—can be placed in perspective, free from the distorting and debilitating structures of conventional narrative art. Those structures, as Mary O'Hare warned in chapter 1, might disguise the pitiful realities of war and cloak them in the trappings of heroism and irony. In terms such as conventional fiction offers, Derby's death would be a bitter tragedy while Vonnegut's survival would be heroic—it would at least grant him the opportunity of portraying himself as a hero. But he has promised Mary that he will not do that, and so *Slaughterhouse-Five* closes with its survivor's guilt intact.

There is no *reason* why twenty-two-year-old Kurt Vonnegut survived the destruction of Dresden. There is no *meaning* for him to discover as he reexamines his circumstances in the affair. The ten succeeding chapters of his novel have proven that in a way that satisfies even the most skeptical readers, because they themselves have been participants in the author's struggle to do the best job possible. Yet his failure to write a conventional war novel does not signify that either the war itself or his attempt to write about it have been meaningless, although a lack of expoundable meaning may lie a step or two behind both the historical and narrative events. To project an opinion of reason or meaning would be to color those events with his own prejudices; if anything, *Slaughterhouse-Five* remains as nonjudgmental as any human work can be. Instead, all presuppositions have been set aside, even the most fundamentally obvious ones of time and space, so that the imaginative experience of working with the Dresden materials can happen with as few intrusions as possible.

What Vonnegut confronts at the end of his book is himself. He works shoulder to shoulder with Bernard O'Hare (from chapter 1) and Billy Pilgrim (from chapters 2–9) to exhume the dead and cremate them. He reemphasizes his own occupancy of the novel's narrative voice as that voice tells about the war winding down and springtime returning with its birdsong and leafing-out trees. If there is a monster at the end of his book, it is not the horror of Dresden, for it too passes away as the surviving elements of human, animal, and natural life resume their cycle—a universal toil which takes them only to their eventual, inevitable deaths sometime in the future. Along the way, Vonnegut's act of novel writing has established that when it comes to imaginative experience past, present, and future can be paged through back and forth as easily as a book. Writing in 1968 and publishing in 1969, Vonnegut can even project Billy Pilgrim's death forward to 1976, a date now in the reader's past. At some point in some reader's time frame Kurt Vonnegut himself will also be dead, yet his words in *Slaughterhouse-Five* will be readable in the present tense of their original writing in which the rules of grammar demand that they continue to be read.

The meaning of his book has been its production. Although that act of production has been generated by an event without meaning, its result is as valid as any work of art can be. In 1976, for a deluxe, limited edition of *Slaughterhouse-Five,* Vonnegut cites the ultimate irony of his Dresden story: not that amid the senseless destruction of an entire city one American prisoner named Edgar Derby was apprehended for stealing a teapot, given the elaborate formality of a criminal trial, and executed for his crime according to the terms of a properly established law, but that from the entire action of the raid only one solitary individual derived any profit. Military historians have done their job, and have determined that the attack on Dresden did not destroy significant German resources, disrupt their communications, or sap their will to fight; it did not significantly aid the Russian advance, nor did it accelerate the American armies' drive to the East. Not one concentration camp inmate's fortunes were improved, nor was a single American, British, or Russian life saved. Who was the person who benefitted from the raid? In his 1976 introduction, Kurt Vonnegut names the name that is so apparent from the structure of his book:

> I write this in October of 1976, and it so happens that only two nights ago I saw a screening of Marcel Ophul's new documentary on war crimes, "The Memory of Justice," which included movies, taken from the air, of the Dresden raid—at night. The city appears to boil, and I was down there somewhere.
>
> I was supposed to appear on stage afterwards, with some other people who had had intimate experiences with Nazi death camps and so on, and to contribute my notions as to the meaning of it all.

Atrocities celebrate meaninglessness, surely. I was mute. I did not mount the stage. I went home.

The Dresden atrocity, tremendously expensive and meticulously planned, was so meaningless, finally, that only one person on the entire planet got any benefit from it. I am that person. I wrote this book, which earned lots of money for me and made my reputation, such as it is.

One way or another, I got two or three dollars for every person killed. Some business I'm in.[22]

# 5

# What Do You Say about a Massacre?

As a famous writer and as a notable public spokesman on any number of social, political, and moral issues, Kurt Vonnegut can find no more to say about Marcel Ophul's cinematic vision of the Dresden holocaust than he could as a relatively unknown writer in 1968 when faced with his jumbled memories and absolutely blank mindscreen when it came to the firebombing itself. As he asks his own publisher in chapter 1, what do you say about a massacre? "Everything is supposed to be very quiet after a massacre, and it always is, except for the birds" (17/19), the author reports to Seymour Lawrence, the successful businessman who has paid him $25,000 to put his experience into words. And what the birds say is not only verbally meaningless, but is phrased as a question itself.

Vonnegut remains mute about the firebombing in 1976 when he is expected to speak about it to the audience of Ophul's *The Memory of Justice*. But he is also speechless about the specifics of the bombing in *Slaughterhouse-Five*, for among its fifty thousand words the reader will not find a single description of the bombing. Throughout the book we know it is coming, for Vonnegut has introduced the topic on the novel's second page; and we know it has happened within the structure of the book, because its final chapter ends with the author and his created

44

characters working in the ruins. But the historical events that transpired on the night of 13–14 February 1945 are nowhere to be found in *Slaughterhouse-Five*. Instead, its fifty thousand words surround a silence, enveloping the unspeakable act of destruction Kurt Vonnegut witnessed in an imaginative framework that tells us as much about the massacre as we can ever hope to know. The author's motive is justifiable, because to reduce this unparalleled catastrophe to the rational limits of language would be to diminish its magnitude and convey the false belief that its reality is somehow manageable. To do that would be to delude readers into thinking that the children's crusade of World War II was not really so bad at all, and that future wars could be just as manageable—exactly what Mary O'Hare fears a conventional writing of Vonnegut's war novel will accomplish.

In 1966, when in residence at the University of Iowa to teach in the Writers Workshop and concentrate on writing the novel based on his wartime experiences, Vonnegut did in fact publish a straightforward account of the bombing raid. It serves as the new Introduction to the hardcover reprint of his novel *Mother Night,* which first appeared in early 1962 as a paperback original. *Mother Night* itself had been anything but straightforward, for its first publisher had taken advantage of Vonnegut's oblique approach to his materials in order to present the book as "An American traitor's astonishing confession—mournful, macabre, diabolically funny—written with unnatural candor in a foreign death cell."[23] This cover notice enfolded not a conventionally presented novel but another series of oddball apparatuses: first an Editor's Note signed by Vonnegut and describing in exquisite detail the practices he has used in editing the purported transcripts of a war criminal's diaries, then Vonnegut's rededication of the man's text, and finally the text itself which appears with its own title page, "The Confessions of Howard W. Campbell, Jr." For the 1966 edition, Vonnegut sought to clarify things by talking about himself not as a supposed editor (which had made him a fictitious character within his own textual apparatus) but as the real-life author of the novel *Mother Night,* now living in Iowa City and ready to talk about his own involvement in the "Nazi monkey business" that *Mother Night* fictionalizes. Back home in Indiana, he recalls, news about the political changes taking place in Germany during the 1930s had come to him as texts, including a copy of *The Protocols of the Elders of Zion* circulated by a local fascist and a wedding license a former resident had to mail home from Hitler's Reich for proof that she had no Jewish blood. "The Indianapolis mayor knew her from high school and dancing school," Vonnegut recalls, "so he had fun putting ribbons and official seals all over the documents the Germans required, which made them look like eighteenth-century peace treaties."[24]

As for his firsthand experiences in the war, they consist of being captured and interned as a prisoner of war; required by the Geneva Convention to work for his keep, Vonnegut willingly accepts the opportunity to avoid imprisonment in the countryside in favor of doing something useful. "I got to go to a city, which was Dresden, and to see the people and the things they did" (vi). This sampling of the quotidian elements in German life during a war that in the United States was being portrayed in images variously heroic, horrific, or cartoonish reflects the texture of *Mother Night,* in which the Nazis are shown not committing atrocities (or even making headlines) but rather going about the mundane tasks of daily life. Reducing an enemy to caricatures, Vonnegut implies, shuts down one's imagination; as a result, the reasons for wars are never given a chance to be understood, for opponents deal with each other in terms of stereotypes and rhetorical figures instead of reality. Interestingly enough, the Dresden firebombing does not appear in the body of *Mother Night,* just as it remains absent from *Slaughterhouse-Five.* But in 1966 Vonnegut feels the need to add his story about that raid to the textual envelope surrounding *Mother Night,* just as for the first edition published four years earlier he had thought it best to describe himself as a fictitious editor:

> There were about a hundred of us in our particular work group, and we were put out as contract labor to a factory that was making a vitamin-enriched malt syrup for pregnant women. It tasted like thin honey laced with hickory smoke. It was good. I wish I had some right now. And the city was lovely, highly ornamented, like Paris, and untouched by war. It was supposedly an "open" city, not to be attacked since there were no troop concentrations or war industries there.
>
> But high explosives were dropped on Dresden by American and

# What Do You Say about a Massacre?

British planes on the night of February 13, 1945, just about twenty-one years ago, as I now write. There were no particular targets for the bombs. The hope was that they would create a lot of kindling and drive firemen underground.

And then hundreds of thousands of tiny incendiaries were scattered over the kindling, like seeds on freshly turned loam. More bombs were dropped to keep firemen in their holes, and all the little fires grew, joined one another, became one apocalyptic flame. Hey presto: fire storm. It was the largest massacre in European history, by the way. And so what?

We didn't get to see the fire storm. We were in a cool meatlocker under a slaughterhouse with our six guards and ranks and ranks of dressed cadavers of cattle, pigs, horses, and sheep. We heard the bombs walking around up there. Now and then there would be a gentle shower of calcimine. If we had gone above to take a look, we would have been turned into artifacts characteristic of fire storms: seeming pieces of charred firewood two or three feet long—ridiculously small human beings, or jumbo friend grasshoppers, if you will.

The malt syrup factory was gone. Everything was gone but the cellars where 135,000 Hansels and Gretels had been baked like gingerbread men. So we were put to work as corpse miners, breaking into shelters, bringing bodies out. And I got to see many German types of all ages as death had found them, usually with valuables in their laps. Sometimes relatives would come to watch us dig. They were interesting too. (vi–vii)

And so the 1966 edition of *Mother Night,* which has become the basis for all subsequent hardcover, paperback, and omnibus editions of this novel, begins with Kurt Vonnegut working not as a textual editor but as an archaeologist of the immediately recent past, unearthing the remnants of a civilization destroyed the night before and learning firsthand how the inhabitants lived and died.

After the war Kurt Vonnegut would study anthropology at the University of Chicago, but his experience at the University of Iowa twenty years later—working not among anthropologists and archaeologists but in the company of a writers' workshop, hammering out the details and texture of fiction rather than fact—prompts him to add this historically accurate piece of firsthand witness to the larger text of an earlier novel, in which the event never figures directly, and to keep it out of the novel he is writing at the time, even though this new book is supposed to be about the event in question. Vonnegut's reasons for adding the Dresden report to *Mother Night* are clear from his introductory comments about the book's moral, and from his concluding notes on its larger ethical dimensions. The 1966 Introduction makes it harder for critics to dismiss *Mother Night* as a flippant response to the Nazi horror, because the author now reveals his credentials as witness and reminds them that the Allies were not immune to racking up atrociously high numbers of innocent deaths themselves. But why he should proceed to write an entire novel centered on this same firebombing and never describe it is a more complex problem to resolve.

An important consideration is that Vonnegut does not feature the actual bombing because he wants to create a predicament. The impetus to his novel's first chapter has been his memory's blank screen when it comes to the central event. The narrative action developing from this flaw allows the author to dramatize his own struggle to write about the war even as he encounters and rejects his culture's preferred ways of speaking about the unspeakable. By not portraying the event itself, the author is able to recast it not as a describable entity but as an unanswerable question: what do you say about a massacre? If the question is a hard one, then the author is absolved from not supplying a simple and satisfactory answer. Instead, he can describe his efforts as a failure and not be blamed for giving up. The question, however, remains, and becomes one asked by the reader as the pages of *Slaughterhouse-Five* are turned and the apparently random jumble of events transpire. Whether the action takes place in Billy Pilgrim's boyhood with his family, in his young manhood (which includes both his wartime service abroad and his optometry studies back home), or in his successful later life, the reader must constantly be wondering about the traumatic experience Billy had at Dresden—for if the living author can have so much trouble with it, what chance does a created character have?

The key achievement of chapter 2 is making Billy's predicament as a character much like Vonnegut's own. Not that Billy is meant to represent the real Kurt Vonnegut—to keep that from happening, the author names himself three times within the succeeding narrative, identifying himself as the POW train is loaded, in the latrine outside the British prisoner camp, and in the boxcar rolling into Dresden, each time distinguishing his particular piece of the action from Billy's. But their responses to the trauma of Dresden and the need for having a response to it are a shared experience. To underscore how common this problem can be, Vonnegut parallels his and Billy's struggles on a more familiar level. Billy Pilgrim, after all, is not portrayed as a novelist trying to draft a novel called *Slaughterhouse-Five* (a metafictional technique favored at the time by younger innovators such as Ronald Sukenick, Steve Katz, and Robert Coover). He does write letters to the newspaper, and disseminates his ideas on a radio talk show, but in these cases the subject is his experience with the Tralfamadorians and their understanding of time, and Vonnegut is careful to characterize these efforts as the actions of a crackpot. Writing a novel is serious business, and while the author denigrates his own attempt and learns to distrust the fraudulent forms of other previously successful literary ventures, he is not inclined to depict the novelist's role as that of a harmless buffoon. But neither does he wish to make Billy's struggle with the matter of Dresden as specialized as a professional author's trouble with writer's block. Instead, Billy's inability to answer an unanswerable question is shown in a scene concerning the death not of hundreds of thousands of people but of just one person, Billy's mother. The result, however, is exactly the same as Vonnegut's inability to answer the question of what all those deaths at Dresden mean.

As Kurt Vonnegut tries to answer his publisher and his readers with regard to a question that overtaxes his limited memory and imagination, Billy Pilgrim finds himself similarly speechless when asked a much more common yet equally unanswerable question by his mother. The time is 1965, and the place is a nursing home where Billy has placed his aged mother (who has caught pneumonia and is not expected to live). He remains the dutiful son, eager to be of whatever help he can and anxious to attend to whatever request she makes. Her question is short, just six words in length, but Vonnegut drags out the scene for most of a page so that just asking this question consumes all of the mother's strength to ask it and most of Billy's and the reader's willing patience to listen. She wants to know "How . . . ?," but cannot go further in the sentence. Like a reader desiring to know what happens next, Billy prompts his mother to complete the grammatical connection and form a complete sentence, which he must have before he can formulate a rational answer. "How *what*, Mother?" he is forced to say, answering her query with another question. Between each line of dialogue Vonnegut inserts more description of their mutually painful efforts to communicate—Billy's mother trying to speak when she cannot, Billy trying to answer when he does not even know the question. Finally, after immense physical labor that taxes her entire body, his mother manages to get the question out. But it is one that neither Billy nor the author can answer: "How did I get so *old*?" (38/44).

Nor can the reader answer such a question, but the inability to do so does not discredit the query or lessen the responsibility to respond. The fact that there *is* no appropriate answer leaves the reader feeling the same emptiness Vonnegut confronts with Dresden and Billy feels with his mother's impending death. This narrative strategy thus defines an absence without having to fill it in with all the considerations that would make it an occupied site—and therefore not an absence any more. Silence is thereby given a voice beyond the physical nature of human articulation.

Vonnegut, Billy, and the reader share the experience of *Slaughterhouse-Five*. It is a partnership the author has formed on the novel's first page when he talks about how he (Kurt Vonnegut, a real-life person) has worked to write a novel (which by definition will have to include fictitious characters, chief among them being Billy Pilgrim) that has turned out to be a radically unconventional work of literary art (which places special demands upon readers trained to read within the traditions of the novel established in English over the past two hundred years). Each element of the partnership is kept on extremely simple terms. Vonnegut portrays himself as a common middle-class American, with habits and practices no more extreme than one might encounter among other married men his age. There is nothing about his self-portrait in chapter 1 to suggest he is an alienated, exotically self-taken writer—to hear him tell it, he is just one more American trying to make an honest dollar. When Billy Pilgrim is introduced in chapter 2, the author again takes pains to present him as unexceptional. He is certainly no hero (Mary O'Hare warned Vonnegut about the pitfalls of creating such roles); and although his pathetic weakness may be overplayed at times, Vonnegut's intention to make him appear as unsoldierly as possible underscores the theme of World War II as a children's crusade undertaken by unprofessional participants with no personal gain in mind. As for the novel's readers, they are never expected to know more than average Americans just like Kurt Vonnegut and Billy Pilgrim. As Vonnegut and Pilgrim do their sincere best to muddle through their assigned tasks as writer and soldier, respectively, the reader too is asked only to do what can be reasonably expected: to see the author struggling with Dresden, to see Billy caught speechless at his mother's bedside, and to realize that no person's life is immune to such trauma, given the fact that men and women are born of mortal parents and are mortal themselves.

Vonnegut's inability to articulate the massacre at Dresden and the impossibility Billy faces in trying to answer his mother's question form what philosophers call a double proof: explaining an abstract metaphysical principle by making reference to an equivalent condition in the natural world. Billy Pilgrim serves as a useful character for making the second part of such double proofs, because he is so thoroughly commonplace in everything he does. Even when his intergalactic travels begin with the Tralfamadorians, Vonnegut is careful to establish that the same things have been happening to Billy in his ordinary daily life. Here again, Vonnegut's technique of making reference to the experience of reading makes the situation fully explicable to even the most traditional readers. Vonnegut as self-present writer restricts himself to chapters 1 and 10, so that he can be counted in the middle chapters as just another soldier. But to keep Billy's adventures parallel to the acts of writing and of reading, Vonnegut introduces a fictitious writer named Kilgore Trout whose novels and short stories provide a running commentary on what would otherwise be the mundane facts of Billy's life.

Consider one of Trout's texts summarized in chapter 5, *Maniacs in the Fourth Dimension:* "It was about people whose mental diseases couldn't be treated because the causes of the diseases were all in the fourth dimension," the reader is told, "and three-dimensional Earthling doctors couldn't see those causes at all, or even imagine them" (90/104). A plot line such as this touches both the Tralfamadorian nature of Billy Pilgrim's time-travel adventures and Kurt Vonnegut's own struggles to articulate the unspeakable. The theme of elusive answers existing in an as yet unreachable fourth dimension is an intriguing possibility, and is propoundable in terms of science fiction adventure and also in terms of self-conscious aesthetics. But as such both Billy's and Vonnegut's problems run the risk of appearing alien to the average reader, who probably is not a novelist and certainly not a space traveler. Therefore Vonnegut puts Billy through a fourth-dimensional experience as exotic as anything Kilgore Trout could imagine and the Tralfamadorians could actually pull off: he lets his hapless character get drunk at a party and then foolishly try to drive home.

The scene is one of nearly total disorientation, but of the style any middle-class American could experience. The occasion is a 1961 New Year's Eve party—a carnivalesque event during which atypical behavior is the norm and conventional rules of good behavior are suspended. Billy drinks a lot, which is expectable for such a party but which by his own standards is unusual, "because the war had ruined his stomach" (40/46). He finds himself doing something else for the first and only time: being unfaithful to his devoted, loving wife. These details are glossed over, as befits their unrepresentative nature. "Somewhere in there was an awful scene," the narrative reports, "with people expressing disgust for Billy and the woman, and Billy found himself out in his automobile, trying to find the steering wheel" (40/46–47).

At this point Vonnegut introduces a carefully plotted and exquisitely detailed account of Billy's search, a narrative much more specific than the party scene and much more instructive than the messy facts of drinking and adultery. Intent upon escaping from all this embarrassment and driving himself home, the inebriated character is shown windmilling his arms, vainly hoping to locate the steering wheel by blind luck. "When that didn't work," as we expect it will not, "he became methodical, working in such a way that the wheel could not possibly escape him" (40/47). The reader is then taken on a patient, deliberate journey from the left-hand door of the car (where the driver would sit) across the seat, as Billy studies each successive square inch of space in front of him. This search takes forty-seven words to recount—a long stretch according to the standards of brevity and conciseness Vonnegut has established for *Slaughterhouse-Five,* and an enormity compared to the quick narrative brush-off given the supposedly lurid details of Billy's discovery with the woman. Given the amount of time and space devoted to this portion of the account, Vonnegut's readers should expect the steering wheel to turn up at the end of it, for with this foolproof methodology, how can Billy now fail? But fail he does, winding up "hard against the right-hand door" (41/47) with the wheel nowhere in sight. At this point the reader feels as dumbfounded as Billy, and might even be tempted to agree with him as he concludes that someone has stolen it.

These are Billy's final thoughts as he passes out and the paragraph ends. But with his patented method of adding single-sentence paragraphs as a way of making an editorial comment, Vonnegut has one more line to write before still another paragraph finds Billy being shaken awake somewhere else. As opposed to the lengthy description of Billy's dedicated search, this paragraph is only eighteen words long, but it articulates what Billy in his drunken struggles never has a prayer of knowing: "He was in the back seat of his car, which was why he couldn't find the steering wheel" (41/47). Although the scene is familiar enough to anyone who drinks too much and tries to drive, its explanation is the same as Kilgore Trout's most exotic science fiction and Kurt Vonnegut's most artistically self-conscious metafiction: Billy and the reader have been misplaced in a different dimension of automotive engineering, through no fault of their own undertaking a systematic search for a steering wheel that simply is not there.

Hence the double proof that makes a theory such as four dimensions of reality as understandable as sitting half-crocked in the back seat of one's car, and which makes a writer's attempt to answer an unanswerable question as intimately felt as the void any person can expect to feel when faced with his or her mother's death. Throughout the early chapters of Billy's adventures Vonnegut singles out several experiences that reflect on his own and his readers' trials with the words of this book. The fact that Billy "time travels" is no more exceptional than what happens to any moviegoer who settles back and becomes one with the shifting time frame of film. Whether conventional or experimental, all movies are physically expressed in an ongoing present tense; unlike the grammar of language, which allows a wide variation among present, past, and future—including such refinements as past perfect for actions that have been already accomplished in the past, subjunctive for a hypothetical action, and optative for actions one hopes will develop—film passes before the viewer's eyes as a continual present. When the action on the screen pertains to historical action in, for example, the year 1588, the year *becomes* 1588 for the attentive audience, even though those events of three centuries ago on the wild seas off Ireland are a world away from an American cinema in 1989. Films, of course, can benefit greatly from such techniques as flashbacks and flashforwards, but even when these events, which are past or future in relation to the movie's "present" time, have to be portrayed as taking place in a physical present, for such is the medium of film that it can only show action as it happens and space as it is being occupied at the moment.

Therefore when Billy Pilgrim is introduced, the first thing revealed about him is that he is living in what appears to be a movie. Within the first pages of chapter 2 all the pertinent details about his life are listed in a fashion befitting *Who's Who,* including date and place of birth, education, military service, marriage, children, profession, and medical history. Interpolated with these milestones of life are the more colorful details of character such as his comical body shape as a child and young man, the secret to his business success, and the trouble he had for a time with his son. Within these three pages Vonnegut goes as far as to sketch out the premise for his novel's entire action: that Billy has begun writing apparently crackpot letters to the local newspaper and appearing on a late night radio talk show, insisting that he has been kidnapped by extraterrestrials and told about a wonderfully liberating concept of time. Here again are the polar extremes of Vonnegut's narrative scope, for his readers are given a thoroughly unexceptional character who begins acting in a ridiculously exceptional manner, a process that takes the readers from the banalities of humdrum middle-class life to the extraordinary possibilities of life in outer space. To bridge this gap Vonnegut proposes the idea of time travel. Indeed, it is the first thing readers are told about Billy as chapter 2 begins: he is "unstuck in time" with "no control over where he is going next," living in a "constant state of stage fright . . . because he never knows what part of his life he is going to have to act in next" (20/23). He will walk through one door in 1955 and come out of another one in 1941, then return through that same door and find himself in a third time and place.

The terms Vonnegut uses to describe Billy's state are specific and interrelated. As a character, he has no control over where or when he is acting. These acts, however, take place in a continual present, because even though on one side of a door it can be 1955 and on the other side 1941, Billy experiences both sides as the present. There is no chronology to these scenes, for Billy never knows how far into the past he will be travelling or even if a scene might include his future (readers will learn later that Billy experiences his death in the future year of 1976 several times, even though the novel's ostensible present is 1968). The manner in which Vonnegut characterizes Billy's condition is not self-explanatory, but neither is it a mystification pulled off with the tricks of science fiction space opera, because the Tralfamadorians are not introduced as an explanation until after readers have been given Billy's complete biography and character sketch—and even then, the outer space business is introduced as the subject of a disoriented individual's letter to the editor and ramblings on a talk show devoted not to facts of life but to the future of the novel. Instead, the author has been careful to describe Billy's condition as identical (if the reader so investigates it) to what an actor in a movie would experience as the film was being made and what a cinema audience would see during the finished product's projection. Consider the out-of-sequence shooting scheduled by most productions, in which the end and parts of the middle of a film may be shot (because of weather, location, and other logistical concerns) before the beginning; one can then appreciate Billy's "stage fright" at the apparent disorder of his life as a character. Also consider how even after the shooting schedule has been completed and the film editor has spliced together all the footage to be used, there still may be violations of strictly historical chronology that will nevertheless appear before the viewer as an action in film's mechanically necessary present tense. With film as the dominant artistic medium in Vonnegut's lifetime and with the complementary techniques of television shaping the imaginations of the generation of readers who would purchase millions of his books in the quarter century beginning with their paperback reissues in the mid-1960s, his portrayal of Billy Pilgrim's condition is hardly atypical. That it is the very first thing he tells readers about the novel's central character is instructive, for it alerts his audience as to how the unfolding action is to be received: not as bizarre fantasy encompassing improbable or outright impossible events, but as a narrative couched within the most familiar terms of middle-class American life and expressed in the artistic style of its most familiar expressive media.

Kurt Vonnegut's own attitude toward science fiction remains as skeptical as that of most readers in the American mainstream. As early as his second novel, *The Sirens of Titan* (1959), he can be found taking pleasure in joking with the paraphernalia that dyed-in-the-wool science fiction addicts take so seriously. In that novel Tralfamadorians are introduced for comic relief—a very dark comedy, to be sure, but obviously in a role that calls into question the self-anointed seriousness that characterizes the brainy, idea-laden works of such science fiction regulars as Robert Heinlein, Arthur C. Clarke, and especially Hal Clement, a physics teacher who quarreled with another writer over whether Martians, with their limited air supply, should be portrayed with big or small noses—a deadly serious debate that led to twenty years of enraged silence between these former best of friends. In *Slaughterhouse-Five* Vonnegut's space people are described just as they are in his earlier novel: not as exotically awesome creatures who stretch readers' imaginations to untold dimensions, but as funny little shafted figures, two feet tall and standing on green suction cups—looking for all the world like that most familiar and unglamorous of earthling devices, the plumber's helper. Their philosophy of time is equally surprising, not in terms of its mental intricacy but because its very freshness of approach reminds readers of something they should have known all along: that time is not a systematic progress of events, marching forward in orderly lockstep, but is in fact a fluid and flexible range of moments that can switch around. Even Billy strives to explain their interpretation with a familiar metaphor. "All moments, past, present, and future, always have existed, always will exist" (23/27), Billy says in his second letter to the editor of the Ilium *News Leader*. He pictures this view of time as looking at the Rocky Mountains from a distance and being able to distinguish one or another stretch, and to focus on this or that peak at will. With time considered as being like the mountain range, one can appreciate how permanent any particular moment is, and how an interesting moment can be dwelt upon. Memory and anticipation are two other apt metaphors, but once again cinema provides the best equivalent of such mobility across all time frames as expressed in a timeless present.

Billy's motive in proselytizing this understanding of time is generous. He wants to comfort his fellow human beings, to relieve them of the unbearable and in his view unnecessary bondage to the inexorability of conventional time. Within their present dispensation, it is inevitable that people be caught speechless when confronted with death—whether of hundreds of thousands in Dresden, or of their own mother back home. Billy provides a text for them to repeat in the face of death, and thereby grants them the gift of articulation. He disseminates this text in the most familiar and even low-brow of manners, as a letter to the editor in his local newspaper. The apparently chronological progression of time as understood on earth is only an illusion, he explains. Events in time are not like beads on a string passing before us, here for a moment and then gone forever, just as life itself seems to pass away. The interpretation he has learned is entirely different: "When a Tralfamadorian sees a corpse," Billy explains to his readers, "all he thinks is that the dead person is in bad condition in that particular moment, but that the same person is just fine in plenty of other moments." Therefore he can say something about death while other people remain speechless: "I simply shrug and say what the Tralfamadorians say about dead people, which is 'So it goes'" (23/27).

Billy's corrective phrase is the same as Vonnegut's, which has been voiced on the book's first page and will be spoken ninety-nine times before its final repetition near the very end. As narrator, Vonnegut says it a self-conscious ninety-nine times, but it is Billy's formulation to his reader that makes possible the significant number of one hundred. And once again, it is part of Vonnegut's double-proof methodology, because while

Vonnegut learns his lesson about reacting to death by reading the works of Louis-Ferdinand Céline and expresses that understanding in an introduction to three of Céline's novels, Billy picks it up from science fiction lore and professes it in the letters column of his hometown newspaper. Moreover, while Vonnegut functions as a writer (someone an average American will rarely meet in person or find living next door), Billy works in that most familiar of professions, optometry. He even sees his dissemination of Tralfamadorian philosophy to be a metaphorical extension of his daily work: "He was doing nothing less, now, he thought, than prescribing corrective lenses for Earthling souls. So many of those souls were lost and wretched, Billy believed, because they could not see as well as his little green friends on Tralfamadore" (25/29). Which brings readers back to Vonnegut's nuts-and-bolts approach to his own job as novelist, because in his next novel, *Breakfast of Champions,* he takes a similar view toward the standard conventions of fiction he has been struggling to overturn, just as Billy has been working to correct the misdirected vision of his patients:

> As I approached my fiftieth birthday, I had become more and more enraged and mystified by the idiot decisions made by my countrymen. And then I had come suddenly to pity them, for I understood how innocent and natural it was for them to behave so abominably, and with such abominable results: They were doing their best to live like people invented in story books. This was the reason Americans shot each other so often: It was a convenient literary device for ending short stories and books.
>
> Why were so many Americans treated by their government as though their lives were as disposable as paper facial tissues? Because that was the way authors customarily treated bit-part players in their made-up tales.
>
> And so on.
>
> Once I understood what was making America such a dangerous, unhappy nation of people who had nothing to do with real life, I resolved to shun storytelling. I would write about life. Every person would be exactly as important as any other. All facts would also be given equal weightiness. Nothing would be left out. Let others bring

order to chaos. I would bring chaos to order, instead, which I think I have done.

If all writers would do that, then perhaps citizens not in the literary trades will understand that there is no order in the world around us, that we must adapt ourselves to the requirements of chaos instead.

It is hard to adapt to chaos, but it can be done. I am living proof of that: It can be done.[25]

Vonnegut's reformulation of the novel, in the midst of *Breakfast of Champion*'s narrative action, is much like Billy's correction of what he calls "Earthling vision." But to make the double proof complete within the limits of *Slaughterhouse-Five,* the author brings in Kilgore Trout to write a science fiction tale propounding the same belief. It is titled *The Gospel from Other Space,* and suggests that the Crucifixion story has proven ineffective because all it teaches is that there will be all hell to pay if the person crucified has connections. Far better, Trout suggests, to reformulate the liturgy so that the crucifiers are condemned for having tortured and killed just an average person—or better yet, a below average person presumed to be comparatively disposable. If that were done, the next two thousand years of Christian history might prove more humane than the last two thousand.

With Kurt Vonnegut, Billy Pilgrim, and Kilgore Trout all dedicated to the same restructurings of their professions, *Slaughterhouse-Five* can function as a rehabilitation of the novel itself. That something needs to be done to revive its ability to speak for our times is obvious. The radio talk show Billy visits is devoted to the future of the novel, a topic being debated in the 1960s by critics who felt the traditional forms of fiction had exhausted themselves and were now unable to represent the concerns of present-day reality in the way Dickens wrote about nineteenth-century London or Balzac chronicled the affairs of Parisian society. In a famous commentary first published in 1961 and cited throughout the decade as an index of the conventional novelist's precarious situation, Philip Roth recalls his own graduate student days at the University of Chicago when the local papers were running stories much like the one Vonnegut describes himself filing in chapter 1. Roth's point is similar to

Vonnegut's: that with their emphasis on characterization, irony, and symbolic action, the newspapers' efforts to break colorful stories were replacing fiction's sense of wonder with a more appealing presentation of fact. The specific story Roth discusses concerns the disappearance and murder of two teenage girls. The police report gives all the necessary facts, "but then the newspapers took over,"[26] running impressionistic drawings of the young women that portray them in the styles of popular comic strip heroines and stationing a reporter on the mother's front porch, from which weekly human interest columns can be issued with the serial effect of a new Charles Dickens installment novel. As the reporters uncover new evidence (which is in fact just more lurid sensationalism coupled with homely "just average people" reactions), the narrative grows to stupendous proportions, generating even more texts, including press conferences hosted by the principals and even a popular song about the purported murderer. Charitable contributions roll in, allowing the mother to furnish a new kitchen and buy two parakeets (whom she names after her murdered daughters).

"And what is the moral of the story?" Roth asks. His answer includes the same shrug-of-the-shoulders attitude that characterizes Vonnegut's response to the question of what do you say about a massacre:

> Simply this: that the American writer in the middle of the twentieth century has his hands full in trying to understand, describe, and then make *credible* much of American reality. It stupefies, it sickens, it infuriates, and finally it is even a kind of embarrassment to one's meager imagination. The actuality is continually outdoing our talents, and the culture tosses up figures almost daily that are the envy of any novelist. Who, for example, could have invented Charles Van Doren [a figure in a television game show scandal]? Roy Cohen and David Schine [principals in the prosecution of Julius and Ethel Rosenberg for revealing secrets of the atomic bomb]? Sherman Adams and Bernard Goldfine [persons involved in the Eisenhower administration's biggest scandal]? Dwight David Eisenhower? (120)

What Philip Roth characterizes as the inability of novelists to speak, because events of their own day were outrunning their talents to describe, journalists would defend as their own newly won turf. In fact, as Vonnegut was searching for ways to write a novel about the central event in his own times, a new genre of literary prose was being invented: the nonfiction novel, also known as the new journalism, which took the very conventions of the traditional novel that fiction writers were discarding as inadequate and used them to describe reality instead. In *The Death of the Novel and Other Stories* Ronald Sukenick had mockingly thrown these familiar writing techniques away, arguing that they had been philosophically and theologically discredited:

> Fiction constitutes a way of looking at the world. Therefore I will begin by considering how the world looks in what I think we may now begin to call the contemporary post-realistic novel. Realistic fiction presupposed chronological time as the medium of a plotted narrative, an irreducible individual psyche as the subject of its characterization, and, above all, the ultimate, concrete reality of things as the object and rationale of its description. In the world of post-realism, however, all of these absolutes have become absolutely problematic.
>
> The contemporary writer—the writer who is acutely in touch with the life of which he is part—is forced to start from scratch: Reality doesn't exist, time doesn't exist, personality doesn't exist. God was the omniscient author, but he died; now no one knows the plot, and since our reality lacks the sanction of a creator, there's no guarantee as to the authenticity of the received version. Time is reduced to presence, the content of a series of discontinuous moments. Time is no longer purposive, and so there is no destiny, only chance. Reality is, simply, our experience, and objectivity is, of course, an illusion. Personality, after passing through a phase of awkward self-consciousness, has become, quite minimally, a mere locus for our experience.[27]

What Sukenick as novelist discards, a feature reporter such as Tom Wolfe is eager to embrace. In the introduction to his anthology that named the subgenre, *The New Journalism,* Wolfe describes how when he came to New York City in the 1960s to write for the legendary *Herald Tribune,* "the most serious, ambitious and, presumably, talented novelists had abandoned the richest terrain of the novel: namely, society, the social tableau, manners and morals, the whole business of 'the way we live now,' in Trollope's phrase." Surveying the style of fiction being pioneered by Sukenick, he sincerely regrets that "There is no novelist who will be remembered as the novelist who captured the Sixties in America, or even in New York, in the sense that Thackeray was the chronicler of London in the 1840's and Balzac was the chronicler of Paris and all of France after the fall of the Empire." Balzac, of course, had felt honored to be "the secretary of French society," but Wolfe believes that "Most serious American novelists would rather cut their wrists than be known as 'the secretary of American society.'" And so the new style of feature journalist takes the job for himself, accepting the fact that "who wants such a menial role?"[28]

But a menial role is not what Vonnegut chooses for himself in drafting *Slaughterhouse-Five*—Tom Wolfe's way of saving the novel by transforming it into journalism is not for him. The approach he uses is actually more like Sukenick's. Not the Sukenick of *The Death of the Novel and Other Stories,* intent upon tearing down the no longer functional conventions of traditional fiction, but rather the Ronald Sukenick committed to rebuilding the novel as an artistic vehicle adequate to postmodern times. It is not a question of innovation versus tradition, Sukenick explains, because the novel *is* innovation. As "the most fluid and changing of literary forms," its responsibility is to respond to immediate experience, and therefore the greatest danger it faces is getting frozen into a particular model. When this happens, "it becomes literary," and loses its readers because "people no longer believe in the novel as a medium that gets at the truth of their lives."[29] But when a particular form is no longer adequate to capture this experience, writers should not pack up the methodology of this form and rename it "the new journalism," because there remains "a fundamental distinction between fiction and data":

> The great advantage of fiction over history, journalism, or any other supposedly "factual" kind of writing is that it is an expressive medium. It transmits feeling, energy, excitement. Television can give us the news, but fiction can best express our response to the news. No other medium—especially not film—can so well deal with our strongest and often most intimate responses to the large and small

facts of our daily lives. No other medium, in other words, can so well keep track of the reality of our experience. But to do this successfully the novel must continually reinvent itself to remain in touch with the texture of our lives. It must make maximum expressive use of all elements of the printed page, including the relation of print to blank space. It must break through the literary formulas when necessary while at the same time preserving what is essential to fiction: incident, feeling, power, scope, and the sense of consciousness struggling with circumstance. (242)

Sukenick's prescription for a truly contemporary novel is fulfilled in *Slaughterhouse-Five.* It is especially significant that Kurt Vonnegut accomplishes the task by incorporating the useful elements of other artistic forms, including cinema and the new journalism, without letting them supercede fiction's purpose. He casts Billy Pilgrim's time travels in the form of a movie, yet does not make a movie himself; instead, he draws upon his readers' familiarity with the conventions of film in order to expand his character's fictive range—while still having him remain absolutely credible as a realistic figure. Vonnegut draws upon the historical events of his time: not just World War II and Dresden, but such milestones as the Kennedy and King assassinations and such particulars as Ronald Reagan's 1968 campaign in the Republican primaries and the unique role the Green Berets played as special forces in Vietnam. Yet these events are never the central focus, nor does Vonnegut seek to colorize them with the methods of traditional fiction. Instead, he uses them as complements to his own act of putting words on the page, so that the reader is reminded that the Kurt Vonnegut writing on Cape Cod on a June evening in 1968 is just as real as the Robert Kennedy who addressed a campaign rally in Los Angeles and then was shot and killed, a moment confirmed in historical time by the entire world's news media.

Having tried both forms on their own terms, as a new journalist and as a film writer, Vonnegut prefers to embrace fiction as his natural artistic medium. Prefacing his first collection of personal journalism culled from the pages of such feature magazines as *Esquire, Life, McCall's,* and even the *Rotarian,* Vonnegut pauses to consider to what extent good journalism and good fiction could be the same, yet how fiction remains superior:

> Am I a New Journalist? I guess. There's some New Journalism in here—about Biafra, about the Republican Convention of 1972. It's loose and personal.
>
> But I am not tempted to do much more of that sort of stuff. I have wavered some on this, but I am now persuaded again that acknowledged fiction is a much more truthful way of telling the truth than the New Journalism is. Or, to put it another way, the very finest New Journalism is fiction. In either art form, we have an idiosyncratic reporter. The New Journalist isn't free to tell nearly as much as a fiction writer, to *show* as much. There are many places he can't take his reader, whereas the fiction writer can take the reader anywhere, including the planet Jupiter, in case there's something worth seeing there.[30]

And so in *Slaughterhouse-Five* Vonnegut disavows the journalist's role so that he can transport his character Billy Pilgrim to Tralfamadore via a credible technique he has borrowed from the cinema. But neither can filmmaking alone do the job he wants to do. Following his own scripting of *Happy Birthday, Wanda June* for the movies, his experiences with the production of *Slaughterhouse-Five* as a major Hollywood motion picture, and the broadcast of a television special based on an amalgam of his work, Vonnegut can step back from these experiences with film and video and restate his true allegiance:

> I have become an enthusiast for the printed word again. I have to be that, I now understand, because I want to be a character in all of my works. I can do that in print. In a movie, somehow, the author always vanishes. Everything of mine which has been filmed so far has been one character short, and the character is me.[31]

To keep himself and his fictional characters together, Vonnegut must reinvent the novel's form. To help him do this, he looks back on his previous novels to see how their characters have survived his own twenty-year writer's block with the matter of Dresden. From his first novel, *Player Piano* (1952), he takes the setting of Ilium, New York, the upstate location for the massive corporation known as General Forge and Foundry. From his second novel, *The Sirens of Titan* (1959), he takes the motivating philosophy espoused by the strange little creatures from Tralfamadore. *Mother Night* (1962) provides more setting and characters, this time from Nazi Germany, while *Cat's Cradle* (1963) offers a test case for discussing the hilarious irony of apocalypse as experienced by a writer trying to get the facts. But of immediate importance to the author's reinvention of form are the interests of the two central characters from his fifth and immediately previous novel, *God Bless You, Mr. Rosewater* (1965). They are the whimsical philanthropist, Eliot Rosewater, and the science fiction writer he idolizes, Kilgore Trout. Before Billy Pilgrim's time travels can proceed too far, Rosewater and Trout are introduced to textualize the novel's experience. In doing so, they join the Tralfamadorians in coaching Billy on the forms of postmodern fiction.

# 6

# The Reinvention of Form

When Billy Pilgrim is being kidnapped to Tralfamadore, he asks his captors for something to read during the long transgalactic journey. The one "Earthling" book on board is something they are taking back for deposit in a Tralfamadorian museum as a key artifact of reading habits from this strange and distant planet. The volume is not one most critics would consider a classic, akin to masterpieces our own age has preserved from previous epochs, such as *The Iliad, The Oydssey,* or *The Aeneid,* nor is it a major religious text like the Bible or the Koran. Most certainly it is not a classic of American letters along the lines of *Moby-Dick* or a cornerstone of literary modernism by any number of authors the Tralfamadorians could have chosen: James Joyce, Virginia Woolf, William Faulkner, or Gertrude Stein. It is not even a contemporary high-brow novel by one of America's Nobel laureates, Saul Bellow or Isaac Bashevis Singer. Instead, it is 1968's version of a shabby commercial best-seller, the type of book that panders to indiscriminate fascination with sex, drugs, and the life-styles of the flashily rich and famous: Jacqueline Susann's *Valley of the Dolls.*

On the one hand, the Tralfamadorians are acting like responsible anthropologists by selecting the era's most popular book. On the other hand, Vonnegut uses this same section of his own novel (chapter 5) to introduce his own critique of fiction's traditional form, to which—despite its grubby subject matter and infantile thematics—*Valley of the Dolls* remains true. As Billy reads it, he is reminded of "the same ups and downs over and over again" (75/87) that characterize the plot lines of realistic fiction. When he pleads for something else, the Tralfamadorians advise him that he is unprepared to read their own fiction, but they do give him some examples of it to satisfy his curiosity. These novels look as different from *Valley of the Dolls* as does *Slaughterhouse-Five*. In fact, the literary theory Billy's Tralfamadorian captor provides sounds very much like an outline of the reinvented form Kurt Vonnegut uses for his own novel, a book short enough to fit inside Susann's work several times:

> each clump of symbols is a brief, urgent message—describing a situation, a scene. We Tralfamadorians read them all at once, not one after the other. There isn't any particular relationship between all the messages, except that the author has chosen them carefully, so that, when seen all at once, they produce an image of life that is beautiful and surprising and deep. There is no beginning, no middle, no end, no suspense, no moral, no causes, no effects. What we love in our books are the depths of many marvelous moments seen all at one time. (76/88).

What the Tralfamadorian critic describes is nothing less than the overthrow of nearly every Aristotelian convention that has contributed to the novel's form in English over the past three centuries. To make a case for such disruptions, Vonnegut continues with his method of the double proof and shifts the discussion of literary form from the flying saucer travelling at warp speed towards Tralfamadore to a hospital room back on Earth, where in another time frame Billy Pilgrim meets a character from the author's previous novel, *God Bless You, Mr. Rosewater*. In that work Eliot Rosewater had proved himself to be a winsome philanthropist, distressed with the degraded condition suffered by mankind in the increasingly industrialized and technologized twentieth century and devoted to reforming social philosophy so that human beings could be valued not for what they can produce but for what they most simply *are*. As a millionaire, Rosewater could conduct experiments in transforming reality by the infusion of large amounts of money, but as a thinker he discovers that perspectives and interpretations must be changed before life can be permanently improved. To this effect he enlists the aid of a novelist, the same Kilgore Trout who will provide so many textual references in *Slaughterhouse-Five*. In *God Bless You, Mr. Rosewater* Trout proposes a reformation of the social contract no less radical than the Tralfamadorian's reinvention of the novel.

"'The problem is this: How to love people who have no use?'" Trout's question, like Vonnegut's query of what do you say about a massacre, demands a total reorganization of thought before it can be answered. On a social level, Trout makes this proposal in the earlier novel:

> In time, almost all men and women will become worthless as producers of goods, food, services, and more machines, as sources of practical ideas in the areas of economics, engineering, and probably medicine, too. So—if we can't find reasons and methods for treasuring human beings because they are *human beings*, then we might as well, as has so often been suggested, rub them out.
>
> Americans have long been taught to hate all people who will not or cannot work, to hate even themselves for that. We can thank the vanished frontier for that piece of common-sense cruelty. The time is coming, if it isn't here now, when it will no longer be common sense. It will simply be cruel.... Poverty is a relatively mild disease for even a very flimsy American soul, but uselessness will kill strong and weak souls alike, and kill every time.
>
> We must find a cure.[32]

During their hospital room meeting in *Slaughterhouse-Five*, Billy Pilgrim and Eliot Rosewater begin a literary discussion that considers the same human needs and leads to the introduction of Kilgore Trout's works. Changing the American work ethic might seem as impossible as changing the way novels are written and read. But given the challenging notions of time and, later, of free will that Vonnegut's Tralfamadorian characters will introduce, such reformations of social and literary theory fit right in. Behind them all is human need, which everyone present agrees is changing. The ups and downs of sequential narrative have been degraded into trashy entertainment like *Valley of the Dolls,* just as the economic and cultural desolation of Rosewater County, Indiana, in Vonnegut's previous novel casts a pall over the postmodern condition of the American dream.

The year is 1948 and Billy is sharing a hospital room with Eliot Rosewater. Both are veterans, and each has committed himself to psychiatric care because of an inability to live in the outside world. Neither feels his present psychological disorder has been caused by the war, although each has had an unnerving experience: as an infantry captain, Rosewater had shot and killed a fourteen-year-old volunteer fireman, mistaking him for a German soldier (an event detailed in *God Bless You, Mr. Rosewater,* after which Rosewater immediately tries to kill himself), while Billy has witnessed the Dresden massacre and helped construct funeral pyres for the mostly innocent victims. "They had both found life meaningless, partly because of what they had seen in the war," we are told. "So they were trying to re-invent themselves and their universe." Under these conditions, Rosewater introduces Billy to the intertext of *God Bless You, Mr. Rosewater:* the writings of Kilgore Trout, who quickly becomes Billy's favorite author and hence achieves intertextual status (along with Rosewater himself) in *Slaughterhouse-Five.* In this opening scene Rosewater explains how reinventing the universe has traditionally been the job of novelists, and how at one point Fyodor Dostoyevski had achieved an ideal artistic arrangement in *The Brothers Karamazov.* That, however, was before World War II, the war in which Eliot committed an unspeakable act and Billy witnessed an even greater one. And so Dostoyevski's form "isn't *enough* anymore" (87/101). By this point the reader should agree, for Billy and the rest of his culture have remained inarticulate when it comes to the truth of their experiences, while war stories get produced as heroic John Wayne movies and the great realistic tradition of Dostoyevski has deteriorated into Jacqueline Susann's *Valley of the Dolls.*

What Billy and Eliot seek from their doctors are the same things novelists provide: "wonderful *new* lies" sufficiently intriguing to make people "want to go on living" (88/101). The question of lies told for artistic effect is something that has interested Vonnegut throughout his writing career, and in his fourth novel, *Cat's Cradle* (1963), he demonstrates how the depressingly hopeless life on a poor Caribbean island can be transformed into a satisfying, useful existence by giving the people parts to play in a simple ritual they all could understand. The ritual is a fabricated religion—the same device used as an organizing principle in Vonnegut's second novel, *The Sirens of Titan* (1959). Yet while admiring the transformative power that religion shares with psychiatry and art, Vonnegut remains cautious about its destructive power when its arbitrary conventions are taken as naturalized absolutes. In such cases the re-invention of reality accomplished by religion becomes a tyrant rather than a servant; or, even worse, it becomes a vehicle by which the designs of one person can enslave others. In a similar manner, we find the Vonnegut of *God Bless You, Mr. Rosewater* distrusting the clinical explanations for Eliot's madness when they appear too solemnly reductive, just as the determination made by the Freudians during Billy's treatment in 1948—that he is unable to adjust to the world because his father threw him to the bottom of a swimming pool when he was a little boy—seems too narrowly specific, considering the enormity of the psychological dislocation the young man has suffered at Dresden just three years before. As for the prescriptive powers of the novel, Vonnegut regrets their unchecked effect in *Breakfast of Champions,* a lesson first taught to him by Mary O'Hare in the first chapter of *Slaughterhouse-Five.* And so if reality is going to be reinvented through the textual and psychological adventures of Billy Pilgrim, readers can rest assured that, as author, Kurt Vonnegut will be keeping a close and skeptical eye on the proceedings, lest they turn into another degraded product of mass-market control.

The new style of novel is a combination of Billy's time travel adventures and Vonnegut's own posture toward narrating them. The Tralfamadorian novel exists as an ideal literary theory for this work, while Billy's conversations with Eliot Rosewater are attempts at a more practical criticism. For specific examples, there are the various texts of Kilgore Trout. Like the Tralfamadorian fictions, they are characterized as being unreadable—not because of their alien form of dots and blank space, but because of their subliterary quality. It is a given principle of science fiction criticism, repeated by Eliot Rosewater from time to time in both *God*

*Bless You, Mr. Rosewater* and *Slaughterhouse-Five*, that authors who work strictly within this subgenre "couldn't write for sour apples,"[33] but instead are valued for the quality of their ideas. Indeed, the science fiction writer's mind and the enormity of the subjects it entertains swamps his hand's ability to write well-crafted prose; thus, Trout's novels and short stories are rarely quoted intact, but instead are summarized in terms of their intellectual content. As such, they become a virtual imaginary library whose encyclopedic content is available to the reader as if in microform. The advantage works on both ends of the author / reader transaction, for Vonnegut is able to create all the books he would like to write simply by citing them as if they exist, while the reader is able to digest the equivalent of hundreds of novels simply by reading the relatively short book that *Slaughterhouse-Five* itself is.

Tralfamadorian literary theory, Billy and Eliot's talks about the role of fiction in adjusting to life, and Kilgore Trout's summarized texts each contribute to a reinvention of the novel's form, because each confronts an accepted practice of traditional fiction and proposes a specifically new approach. Novels on Tralfamadore are not read sequentially, but all at one time, a practice not only untraditional on Earth but patently impossible; even though a reader could disregard the order of a book's chapters and read them out of order, there is no way one can scan all two hundred or more pages of a book simultaneously. More easy to accomplish in physical terms is the device of Billy and Eliot, as characters in the novel, discussing not just the meaning of life but the purpose of fiction in that life. Such metafictional involvements have been a part of the novel's history from the start, but always as an exception to the mainstream; by the middle of the nineteenth century, the great tradition of suspended disbelief had taken hold among novels written in English, and even the great modernist experiments of the earlier twentieth century (including such radical devices as stream of consciousness narration, automatic writing, and a preponderate emphasis on deep psychology and myth) stopped short of empowering characters within the work to take control of its direction. Although such behavior was occasionally portrayed, as in Flann O'Brien's *At Swim-Two-Birds* (1939) and more frequently in the 1960s with such novels as Robert Coover's *The Universal Baseball*

*Association, J. Henry Waugh, Proprietor* (1968), Ronald Sukenick's *Up* (1968), and Steve Katz's *The Exagggerations of Peter Prince* (1968), these works were branded as "experimental fiction" and overtly excluded from mainstream consideration. It would take Vonnegut's own breakthrough with *Slaughterhouse-Five* before such internal tampering with the business of fiction could become both best-seller material and a subject for academic consideration as a key development within the tradition of the American novel. And as for Trout's science fiction, that subgenre remains somewhat outré, to the extent that throughout his career Vonnegut has complained about being consigned to it as a way of having the serious aspects of his art disregarded. At the same time, he expresses regret that writers can not include the themes and techniques of science and technology in their fiction without being so labeled; an understanding of such subjects is an important part of contemporary life, yet critics trained by English departments preach that what happens across campus in biology, chemistry, and physics are of no account for the novel.

How *Slaughterhouse-Five* achieves the timeless and spaceless dimensions of Tralfamadorian fiction is Vonnegut's major formal achievement, but to accomplish the task he must draw on both the metafictional behavior of Billy Pilgrim and Eliot Rosewater and the science fiction writing of Kilgore Trout. The key to this strategy is labeling Rosewater and Trout as being atypical—completely out of the mainstream—while maintaining Billy's character as solidly within the American middle class. To him, Rosewater and Trout are not ideals to be pursued, but rather unusual sources for new information. They bring an added dimension to Billy's life, just as their philosophies of art and life expand the familiar style of the novel. Because he is an essentially passive person, Billy Pilgrim is able to receive this data and absorb its influence without undergoing violent change. In a similar way, *Slaughterhouse-Five* is able to operate as an experimental novel without recourse to any of the radically combative attitudes Vonnegut's younger colleagues were using to distance themselves from traditional fiction. Like his outer space characters who look like familiar old plumber's helpers, Vonnegut's innovative techniques are drawn from common enough sources, so that the novel he delivers seems more like a part of life than an obvious revolt against it. Indeed, as Mary

O'Hare would say, it is the traditional form of popular storytelling that is unfaithful to life.

Although the name used to describe Billy's adventure sounds complex, Vonnegut makes it clear from the way he uses it that time-travel can be as familiar an experience for his readers as random associations. As a science fiction device, it allows the author to shift scenes with fluid ease, moving from year to year and from place to place with no need for cumbersome exposition to explain such shifts. But the juxtapositions are not made randomly, for as the Tralfamadorian explains about his own planet's fiction, the author chooses them carefully to produce a specific image. To remind his readers how such associations can take place without the exotic business of extraterrestrial time-travel, Vonnegut shows Billy driving his Cadillac through a contemporary scene whose devastation looks like battle scenes in Germany. But instead of time travelling, Billy is simply passing from one part of Ilium, New York, to another: from his affluent suburb to the city's black ghetto that has been destroyed by a recent riot (such as those that did devastate sections of many American cities in 1967). One paragraph later, he is seen driving through "a scene of even greater desolation" where the landscape has been so consumed that it "looked like Dresden after it was fire-bombed—like the surface of the moon" (51/59). Here Vonnegut tempts the reader with two possibilities. Is Billy time traveling to Dresden now? No, for he is still in Ilium, and the year is still 1967. Is Billy seeing even more destruction from the city's civil disturbances? No, for he is now driving through an area of urban renewal. Each transfer of attention, however, has been an example of traveling within time and space; only here the reader, not Billy, has done the travelling, by means of logical association.

There are outright shifts for which the science fiction device is needed, but Vonnegut is careful not to make them more thematically extreme than what he has accomplished in the Ilium ghetto episode. Without the buffering material of expositional machinery, the images from Germany in 1944 are able to stand in immediate proximity to images from the United States in 1967—not just when the physical aspects of riot damage and urban renewal appear as extensive as Belgian towns ravaged by artillery barrages and infantry assaults or even as thorough as the firebombing of Dresden, but when a tear Billy sheds as crippled people, exploited by magazine sales managers, ring his doorbell, is actually caused by the winter wind blowing in his eyes at the Battle of the Bulge. As in the making of metaphors themselves, juxtaposing two different elements can create a third, and producing such an otherwise inexpressible image is what Vonnegut intends to do.

Billy Pilgrim cannot read a Tralfamadorian novel, nor can any Earthling reader. In a 1973 interview, Vonnegut admitted how hard it was to achieve the effect that the Tralfamadorians find so easy, that of seeing a group of distinct moments all at the same time. Asked about the similarity of his formal attempt with those of Donald Barthelme, Ronald Sukenick, and others, he agreed:

> Well, I suppose we're all trying to. One thing we used to talk about—when I was out in Iowa [teaching at the University of Iowa Writers Workshop and beginning *Slaughterhouse-Five*] was that the limiting factor is the reader. No other art requires the audience to be a performer. You have to count on the reader's being a good performer, and you may write music which he absolutely can't perform—in which case it's a bust. Those writers you mentioned and myself are teaching an audience how to play this kind of music in their heads. It's a learning process, and *The New Yorker* has been a very good institution of the sort needed. They have a captive audience, and they come out every week, and people finally catch on to Barthelme, for instance, and are able to perform that sort of thing in their heads and enjoy it. I think the same is true of S. J. Perelman; I do not think that Perelman would be appreciated if suddenly his collected works were to be published now to be seen for the first time. It would be gibberish. A learning process is required to appreciate Perelman, although it's very easy to do once you learn now to do it. Yeah, I think the readers are coming along; that's a problem; I think writers have tried to do it always and have failed always because there's been no audience for what they've done; nobody's performed their music.[34]

The learning process Vonnegut describes had been a patient affair for the readers of Donald Barthelme, who between 1963 and Vonnegut's interview in 1973 had published seventy-five stories in the *New Yorker*, in the process upsetting that magazine's conventional expectations for short fiction and reinventing the genre's form. Barthelme's earliest experiments are among his most whimsical: publishing what his subtitle claims is an entire novel on a single page, a narrative written in the cryptic form of *TV Guide* program notes; drafting another story within the laboratory-and-field-test language of *Consumer Reports;* and producing a concise classic, "Views of My Father Weeping," with the juxtaposition of self-contained paragraphs, much like Vonnegut's jigsaw puzzle of relationships in *Slaughterhouse-Five.*[35]

Like Perelman, Barthelme appreciated how humor could relax the reader's skeptical resistance to new forms. This same approach is evident in Vonnegut's novel: Billy's time-travel stumblings from scene to scene are often portrayed in the manner of hapless slapstick. Even the creation of bright new metaphors by means of these sudden juxtapositions is first of all meant to be funny. Here Vonnegut's compatriot from the younger generation is Richard Brautigan, whose work Vonnegut discovered in small press editions on the West Coast and then brought to the attention of his publishers, Seymour Lawrence and Delacorte Press, who disseminated such novels as *Trout Fishing in America* and *In Watermelon Sugar* to a broad commercial audience. The former novel is Brautigan's funniest—not simply because of the whimsy of its thematic posture or recounted incidents, but because of its gently comic play with the materials of metaphor (implied comparison) and simile (expressed comparison) themselves, the very constructs Vonnegut would achieve by juxtaposing distant times and places through Billy's time-travel. In *Trout Fishing in America* Brautigan teaches his readers how to receive this strange new novel by setting each scene with outlandish comparisons. Consider the cheap hotel where the author wants some action to take place. Rather than simply describe it as shabby and unappealing, with the pervasive smell of Lysol permeating its lobby, Brautigan names the odor and then characterizes it by means of an especially extreme comparison: "The Lysol sits like another guest on the stuffed furniture, reading a copy of the *Chronicle,* the Sports Section." But as if the distance between the disinfectant and the newspaper-reading guest is not great enough, Brautigan follows immediately with another simile, this time visual: "It is the only furniture I have ever seen in my life that looks like baby food."[36] The magnification of distance between the two elements of comparison creates a space in which Brautigan's art can happen. Throughout *Trout Fishing in America* his narrative destabilizes conventional views by defamiliarizing the elements of comparison. The effect achieved is just the opposite of dead language, in which clichéd comparisons lull the readers to sleep; here they are shaken awake and forced to see things with a radical sense of awareness, a condition that allows the author to create a sense of reality beyond that of the everyday world yet not completely alien to it. One can easily find, among the quotidian elements of familiar American life, such things as Lysol, hotel lobby loiterers lost in the sports section of the local newspaper, shabby furniture, and baby food. All are validly existing individual items, but by juxtaposing them in fresh, exciting ways, Brautigan is able to open a new range for the possibilities of understanding. Within this expanded space between the juxtapositions of tenor (the thing to be compared) and vehicle (the object of comparison), a new appreciation is formed. Like Barthelme, Brautigan is extremely patient in teaching his readers how to respond to such techniques, which begin as exposition but soon become the action itself.

Vonnegut, of course, has begun teaching his readers how to read *Slaughterhouse-Five* in his novel's first chapter, which rehearses the special difficulties he encountered in writing this book—difficulties that preclude the delivery to his publisher and readers of a conventionally written work. Billy Pilgrim, his novel's chief character, does not appear until the beginning of chapter 2, so that even before the readers learn about the intricacies of time-travel they are thoroughly familiar with the author's own travels through temporal history and geographical space in search of a method to write his book. And when Billy first appears, the author provides a complete and credible character sketch encompassing everything from his date of birth and details of major personal and professional milestones to the homely business of what he looks like at the present moment: sitting at a typewriter (as the reader has seen Vonnegut in chapter 1 and will meet him again at the novel's end in chapter 10) in the unheated rumpus room of his suburban home, dressed in pajamas and a bathrobe, the cold turning his bare feet "blue and ivory" (24/28).

These colors are noteworthy, for in the chapter's four pages of introductory exposition, they are the first physical details to be recorded. As such, they are likely to remain in the reader's memory, if only subliminally, not just because they are the first colors to be mentioned, but because of their schematic combination. Later on, the boxcars of the prisoner-of-war train transporting Billy and the other captured Americans across Germany toward Dresden are described as being painted orange and black, another scheme which by its combination is fixed mnemonically in the reader's memory. Vonnegut takes care with these colors because they will be used to trigger the reader's own time-travel, as a corpse removed from the train will be characterized by its bare feet, colored blue and ivory, while the caterer's tent at the wedding of Billy's daughter in the year 1967—twenty-three years later in terms of actual history but only two pages apart in Vonnegut's book—will be described as colored orange and black. Because these specific colors are repeated, readers feel the passages belong together, even though they are two hemispheres and nearly a quarter of a century apart in terms of the conventional ordering of time and space. There are many such examples throughout *Slaughterhouse-Five,* making an otherwise apparently random book hang together. It is even better if the reader does not make the association consciously, for then the effect will be subliminal, giving the deep impression that this novel does have a principle of order to it, even if that principle cannot be articulated—just as Vonnegut himself finds it hard to articulate his experience in Dresden, even though there is no question that he was there.

And so the disparate adventures of Billy Pilgrim's time-travels are first of all organized by the principle of visual associations. In the bowels of Carlsbad Caverns, where a tour guide tells the youngster there is no light whatsoever, little Billy sees an eerie glow emanating from the radium dial of his father's wristwatch—the exact same image used years later to describe the pale faces of Russian prisoners of war. Here the associations are only a page apart, where the reader will surely make the connection. But elsewhere in *Slaughterhouse-Five* Vonnegut stretches the physical distance, especially when the time itself is relatively close. In chapter 2, just before Billy is captured, he pauses to rest in the forest, leaning back against a tree in the posture of the reclining corpse encountered by Henry Fleming in the famous scene from Stephen Crane's *The Red Badge of Courage*. Nearly fifty pages later, in chapter 5, Edgar Derby is seen watching over Billy sleeping off his attack of hysteria at the British POW compound—an event just a few days later in regular time. But to bridge the textual gap created by his four dozen intervening pages, Vonnegut gives Derby something to do that will strike a familiar chord in the reader's memory: he passes the time by reading *The Red Badge of Courage*. Thus whether many years of time or many pages of *Slaughterhouse-Five* intervene, the reader is provided with obvious linking devices to hold things together, and is thereby given a lesson in how to associate otherwise radically juxtaposed passages.

Like Donald Barthelme's and Richard Brautigan's teaching methods, Vonnegut's schooling of his readers has taken place within his narrative and by means of fiction's most essential building blocks themselves: words and images. Unlike the more metafictional experiments of Ronald Sukenick, Steve Katz, and William H. Gass, discussions about the construction and purpose of fiction are held to a minimum. They are present in *Slaughterhouse-Five*, but as dialogues between two eccentrics in a mental asylum—a manner of portrayal that gives the reader a valid excuse for regarding this topic as extraordinary, an escape route not provided in Sukenick's novel *Up* and available only as a graphic illustration (the full-page drawing of an emergency exit from the text) in Katz's *The Exagggerations of Peter Prince*. The conversations between Billy Pilgrim and Eliot Rosewater that the reader can listen in on are much like Vonnegut's complaints as an author in chapter 1: not so much about what the new form of novel should do, but what the older styles of fiction can no longer accomplish. The one positive guideline proposed comes from an even more exotic source, the Tralfamadorian who during Billy's kidnapping explains the literary theory behind his planet's form of novel. But by the time this analysis is presented—near the beginning of chapter 5, almost precisely halfway through *Slaughterhouse-Five*—the reader has already been experiencing the simultaneity of otherwise distinct passages, thanks to Vonnegut's verbal and visual linking devices. A scene in Carlsbad Caverns may not make sense by itself, just as the description of the Russian prisoners does not make formal sense by itself. But when the reader notices that a reference to radium wristwatch dials has been made in each passage, a sense of meaning is created—not in one passage or the other, but in an independent space between the two. This is the realm of spontaneous appreciation Vonnegut seeks to achieve, which is the same simultaneity of comprehension that seems so unattainable when described in Tralfamadorian terms. This educational device in turn prepares the reader for an appreciation of other Tralfamadorian notions, such as the fluidity of movement within time and the illusion of there being any real free will, that seem anathema to everything humans believe. In terms of literary technique, what is initially accomplished by the most radical defamiliarization turns out to be a rather familiar notion after all.

Billy's time travels are structured like cinema montages (with immediate linking devices such as a windblown tear or a photographer's flash bulb) and associated with one another on the basis of key words and specific visual images. Billy and Eliot's literary conversations are constructed as critiques of an invalid form of literature, while their yearning for an ideal style of writing is expressed explicitly by an apparently higher authority (from outer space, as generated by the same extraterrestrial civilization that made whimsy of mankind's destiny in *The Sirens of Titan*, directing such mammoth endeavors as the Great Wall of China and the pyramids of Egypt as routine messages to a stranded flying saucer pilot observing Earth from a moon of Saturn). In the meantime, *Slaughterhouse-Five* has taken shape as a Tralfamadorian novel within the reader's hands, as from page to page its associations are formed on the levels of language and image rather than just from chronological history and theme. For thematic innovations, Vonnegut turns to the self-conscious textualization of an invented writer's work. Kilgore Trout is introduced as Eliot Rosewater's favorite author, and he soon becomes an immense comfort to Billy, providing the service that more traditional authors cannot. He is not from outer space, but he writes about it; more specifically, he views the matters of Earth from an outer space perspective, thereby restructuring subjects and themes that have gone stale in the hands of conventional writers. By the time that Vonnegut's readers have been trained in the new methods necessary to appreciate Kilgore Trout, an entire library of his work is provided in summary form, expanding the dimensions of *Slaughterhouse-Five* with a thematic reinvention complementary to its formal achievement.

When Kilgore Trout appears at the end of *God Bless You, Mr. Rosewater,* it is to validate his texts that Eliot has been citing and that the larger narrative has been summarizing; brought into the dramatic action itself to tell blustery old Senator Rosewater why his philanthropist son has become insane, Trout fills the novel's closing pages with a direct lecture on postmodern America's need for a transformed social philosophy. In *Slaughterhouse-Five* his role is more delicate. As Billy's time travels create a new awareness in the reader by forcing together narrative incidents that would otherwise be safely insulated from one another by means of chronological time and geographical space (not to mention the physical separation induced by the many intervening pages a conventionally written novel would provide), Trout's offbeat themes and wackily construed situations expand Vonnegut's own narrative from within. Thus not only is a relatively short novel like *Slaughterhouse-Five* greater than the sum of its parts, its internal features are larger than the forms that encase them. A typical Vonnegut sentence can be caustically brief—sometimes just one word—while a paragraph can be as short as one sentence. But when a Vonnegut sentence summarizes a two-hundred-page Trout novel, or when a paragraph in *Slaughterhouse-Five* runs through a virtual anthology of Trout's shabby little science fiction stories, the reader's world of reference is multiplied exponentially—a formally implosive technique of Vonnegut's fictive form falling in upon itself, only to explode outward with a rich multiplicity of meaning. When Kilgore Trout himself steps into *Slaughterhouse-Five* as a character, it is not simply to propound theories as the author's spokesperson but to take an integral part in the narrative action.

Trout's function as an author is discussed by Eliot and Billy in chapter 5; his novels and stories are introduced in summary form within the pages immediately following. By the time the man himself appears, the reader is familiar with both the theory and practice of his work. His placement in chapter 8, however, is strategic, for he does much more than preach to the choir about themes Vonnegut's novel has already established. The context in which he appears is significant, because it figures within the formal structure of Billy Pilgrim's time travelling. The chapter begins with another character brought in from a previous Vonnegut novel, Howard W. Campbell, Jr., of *Mother Night.* In that novel Campbell functions as a complex, multiform construction: a double-agent whose own identity has been lost amid the uses contending political forces have made of him. Here in *Slaughterhouse-Five* only one dimension can be seen, that of the diehard Nazi propagandist, whose techniques are for once ineffective as Edgar Derby talks him down with a textbook lecture on American patriotism and virtue. Derby's words, however, are drowned out by the air defense sirens of Dresden, announcing a false alarm just one night before the fateful raid. This night, as Billy sleeps in his meat locker quarters, he dreams of Kilgore Trout: specifically, his daughter's dismay at Trout's influence, which we now learn she has voiced "in the argument . . . with which this tale began" (142/165), although that part of their conversation is saved until now—another instance of spatial reshaping via time-travel. Then, in the next episode, one that according to conventional chronology would feature the next day's fatal firebombing, the scene shifts away from Billy's night in Dresden in 1945 and away from his time-travel dream of a conversation in Ilium, New York, during 1968, to the time in 1964 when Billy meets Kilgore Trout. Thus Trout appears at what would in traditional form be the novel's climax, the destruction of Dresden.

His behavior in this chapter accomplishes in structural terms what a realistic account of the bombing would do for conventional thematics: it justifies the novel's form and articulates its central statement. His appearance comes as a matter of time-travel, and is spatially juxtaposed with Billy's presence in the Dresden slaughterhouse. It is prepared for by Howard Campbell, the protagonist of Vonnegut's earlier novel who now, in the manner of a repertory theater's cast member, plays a supporting role in stating the Nazis' case with regard to America's part in the war. And as Trout begins to act out his own personal role in the business of *Slaughterhouse-Five,* he validates not just the themes and messages of his science fiction testaments but demonstrates the technical side of their employment within Vonnegut's own novel, as the mundane little details of his daily life prompt summaries of novels and stories he has written. Working as a supervisor of newspaper carriers, he cajoles them with the question of whether they think money grows on trees (he has in fact written a novel with just such a plot device—a money tree whose roots are fertilized by the humans who have fought and killed each other for its bounty). He scorns a newsboy who is quitting as a gutless wonder, which allows Vonnegut to summarize another Trout novel, in this case one anticipating the use of napalm by American forces in Vietnam and how employment of such a terrible weapon could be accepted as standard operating procedure. In the simple process of Billy meeting Trout, the narrative of *Slaughterhouse-Five* is twice deepened with references to murderous greed and offhand destruction in a war fought thirty years after the lesson of Dresden should have been learned.

The greatest impact of Trout's appearance as a character is on himself, for as an unknown hack science fiction writer he has been working with absolutely no sense of an audience. "All these years," he tells Billy, "I've been opening the window and making love to the world" (145/169), with no response except one crazed letter he presumes was written by a fourteen-year-old, but who is in fact the wartime killer of a fourteen-year-old civilian fireman, Eliot Rosewater. That exchange of texts—Trout's stories for Rosewater's fan letter—had yielded nothing, but now as Billy introduces him to the ongoing action of *Slaughterhouse-Five* he is able to take on a living role as a writer, as a creatively shaping force in the conduct of human affairs.

His scene consists of just one episode, but it is the one central to the novel's reinvention of form. The occasion is a party celebrating Billy Pilgrim's eighteenth wedding anniversary, a common occasion for spatially collapsing time. Within the framework of this event Trout is able to glory in his role as writer, for as a published author he is the hit of the party. He finds the guests minimally literate and gullible for anything he says, and so he alternately amazes and terrifies a lovely but brainless young woman with advice about how what happens in novels must be factually true, how the substance of his fiction has been things that have happened to him, and that just as he is listening to her now, "God is listening, too. And

*The Reinvention of Form*

on Judgment Day he's going to tell you all the things you said and did"
(147/172) and punish her awfully if she has done badly.

What Trout proposes is a preposterously simple view of fiction, but
one that has maximum moral impact. The young woman is described as
turning gray and being "petrified" (148/172), a posture that recalls
Vonnegut's own self-proclaimed status at the end of chapter 1, where he
sees himself as made into a pillar of salt for looking back at the destruction of Dresden in his past. It anticipates what happens to Billy on the
next page when, after listening to a barbershop quartet entertaining his
party, he nearly collapses, looking like a ghost. What has happened is
that, in Trout's presence, Billy has finally made contact with the heart of
his Dresden experience, the central event eluding him throughout his
time-travels and causing so much trouble to Kurt Vonnegut as he has
struggled to write this book. What has happened is relatively simple: as
the optometrists' quartet group themselves together for the close har-
mony of an old time song, the refrain of which sings of yearning for *"that
old gang of mine"* to whom time dictates that they say *"So long forever,
old fellows and gals, so long forever old sweethearts and pals"* (148/172),
Billy recalls the quartet of German guards in his slaughterhouse prisoner-
of-war quarters struggling to articulate the horror at their first glimpse of
the Dresden holocaust on that February morning in 1945. But Trout's
presence is necessary to make the final confirmation of this connection
between disparate moments in time. Trout's appraisal, like his mocking
of the gullible young woman, is incorrect, for the process he describes—
looking through a time window in order to see the past—is a rationally
mechanical device characteristic of his own hackwork in the subgenre of
space opera. Billy denies it, just as he denies his wife's judgment that he
has seen a ghost. What *has* happened is that he has time travelled once
again, only this time to the key event, the moment of Dresden's destruction, and for the first time is able to articulate it, to *tell a story.* Rather
than being a low-grade science fiction device, part of a hack writer's
chatter to befuddle half-inebriated party guests, time travel is here seen
to be a dignified literary technique. It is the technique that brings Trout
himself into the story, not to spout absurd banalities, but to represent his
own works that have enriched the possibilities and deepened the impact

of Vonnegut's novel. Now he serves in attendance as Billy makes the final decoding of his own textual experience, learning to read the correlative signs between an anniversary party in 1964 and an air raid in 1945 as a way of making his present predicament meaningful to himself—the job fiction is supposed to do all along.

Trout's fiction is greater than his ability, or perhaps his willingness, to seriously analyze and articulate its power, even though he can play with its moral effect. In similar manner, so is Vonnegut's. Throughout *Slaughterhouse-Five* he has made fun of his chief character's bumbling attempts to be a soldier, a husband, a father, and an upstanding member of his community. That just when Billy reaches the security of middle age in comfortably middle-class America he begins to fancy himself a prophet is another of life's ironies. But it is an important one, for just as Mary O'Hare did not want yet another fraudulent portrayal of her own husband and Vonnegut himself as glorious war heroes, Billy is not allowed to become too much of a glorified and self-glorying savant. As Kurt Vonnegut has struggled through the business of chapter 1 and chapter 10, trying to write his novel and then looking back on its unconventional appearance, so has Billy muddled through his wartime and postwar experiences, doing the best he can with the extremely limited resources provided him. When it comes to describing Dresden, it is not in response to Hollywood's lure of great renumeration, bestsellerdom's promise of stature, or even the adulation of other veterans anxious to have their stories told in a grand and heroic manner, as befits the victors of a war. Instead, it is in response to his pregnant mate's request, "Tell me a story" (153/178), as a substitute for the other small favors, such as going out for ice cream and strawberries, that circumstances prevent him from doing. Kidnapped to Tralfamadore and exhibited with another captive, a star of quasi-pornographic movies, Billy is no more removed from the normal conditions of wife, children, and daily work in the real world than was Vonnegut himself—who, to earn money and draft this novel left his home of fifteen years on Cape Cod to teach and write in the extraordinarily isolated and artificial world of the University of Iowa's Writers Workshop in Iowa City. That both storytellers struggle is expectable; it is their honesty about that struggle and self-effacement with regard to its product that distinguishes their work.

Billy's story is plain and matter of fact. It reads much like the 1966 introduction to the new edition of *Mother Night,* complete to the comparisons of bombs walking across the earth's surface like the footsteps of giants and the physical condition of corpses burned down to the size and shapes of small logs. It ends precisely where the author's own self-apparent story ends two chapters later: in a suburb where the abandoned prisoners are bedded down for the night in a manger, before the process of repatriation begins. These scenes are described in loving detail, for they are the stuff of human mercy and kindness. As for the details of the bombing themselves, they are voiced by an intimately expressed characterization of silence: "the four guards who, in their astonishment and grief, resembled a barbershop quartet" (154/179). They, like Vonnegut in real life and like Billy Pilgrim in the action of this novel, are speechless in the face of such enormity. But the temporal and spatial juxtapositions of the human imagination—the key facility that makes humans so superior to beasts—provide the words, even though they are sung years later in a context where their meaning signifies little more than the chordal variations of a song. What matters is that Billy has confronted his memory and employed it in the telling of a plain and honest story, a tale whose simplicity cuts through the obscuring and denaturing conventions that had come to typify war stories in Vonnegut's time.

# 7

# History Transcended

The formal achievement of *Slaughterhouse-Five* is its restructuring of the reading experience. Like the putative Tralfamadorian novel, it allows its readers to come as close as humanly possible to experiencing all of its disparate episodes at once. Because of its briefness and nonchronological order, its effect is not steadily cumulative; its impact is not received as additive and progressive, but rather juxtapositional, as its episodes fragmented in time and space register meaning not so much by themselves but rather in relation to one another. As such, *Slaughterhouse-Five* is a system rather than an entity, a combination of differences rather than identities. This formal achievement befits the special nature of Vonnegut's theme: that the struggle to say something about a massacre is frustrating, because there is really nothing that can be said. What *cannot* be said fills that central void, and constitutes the novel's formal parts.

Articulating the inability to speak can be an eloquent experience for the author and for his central character. Those facts are demonstrated by Vonnegut's persistence in his dedicated writer's role and Billy's exhausting series of time-travels around and about this same matter of Dresden that frustrated his artistic creator for so long. The labors of each, however—the author's exploration of all the different ways to surround the

*History Transcended*

Dresden experience with language, and his character's life taking form as an envelope that contains the unexpressable truth witnessed during the firebombing—form the complementary systems of *Slaughterhouse-Five*, as Kurt Vonnegut and Billy Pilgrim play out the roles given them by fate to the best of their personal abilities. As Vonnegut says in the prologue to his later novel, *Slapstick*, life does seem like the "grotesque, situational comedy" of films by Laurel and Hardy. "There are all these tests of my limited agility and intelligence," the author remarks. "They go on and on." But rather than despair, he admires the response of the two dogged optimists who, in the face of a booby-trapped universe, "never failed to bargain in good faith with their destinies, and were screamingly adorable and funny on that account."[37]

Vonnegut's humor regarding his subject makes it easier for the reader to absorb, yet he never alters its essential nature so that war itself can be laughed away as a harmless exercise. Although all forms of death are leveled to the same reductive condition with the repetitive comment, "So it goes," death still pervades the novel—one hundred deaths, of all forms of life, do appear, an average of ten per chapter, far more separate incidents of death than in even conventional war stories. Painfully honest to his materials, Vonnegut may leave the actual firebombing undescribed, but that is because there can be no human witness to the event itself. Anyone who would have climbed up from his or her deep shelter or ventured in from the distant countryside would have been asphyxiated and incinerated almost instantaneously, with no time to register the event. As to the enormity of that event, it outstrips the individual observer's ability to respond. The ruins go on and on, far beyond one person's ability to see, and the casualties are so great in number that they become just an abstract figure. Hence the author's need to reinvent the novel so that it can encompass something Tralfamadorian readers can do: see everything all at once. The spatial and temporal juxtapositions of *Slaughterhouse-Five* do just this; by frustrating attempts to relate its incidents in any sequentially historical manner, the novel encourages its readers to relax their quest for meaning and reserve all judgments until the end, when its various parts are complete and can be reflected upon as one seamless whole.

Yet history itself is never slighted. In chapter 9, after Billy Pilgrim has met Kilgore Trout and learned to tell his Dresden story and before Kurt Vonnegut himself joins him as a corpse miner in Dresden for the book's final chapter, Billy shares a hospital room with another textual authority. In 1948 his roommate had been Eliot Rosewater, and the texts discussed and debated were the novels and short stories of Kilgore Trout. In 1968, as Billy recovers from an airplane crash, he finds himself in a semiprivate room with a Harvard history professor named Bertram Copeland Rumfoord, currently at work on a history of the U.S. Army Air Corps in World War II. Because Rumfoord needs to review the key historical texts about the war's major bombings and air battles, the reader is treated to a recitation of President Harry Truman's announcement of the atomic attack on Hiroshima and the two prefaces to David Irving's *The Destruction of Dresden,* contributed by the USAF's and RAF's leading strategists, Lieutenant General Ira C. Eaker and Air Marshal Sir Robert Saundby. All three texts justify mass bombardment of civilian populations, a theory of war developed as early as the 1920s by the Italian military theorist General Giulio Douhet and the American aviator General Billy Mitchell. Eaker commanded the U.S. Eighth Air Force, which from bases in England pounded Germany by day; his specialty was devising the long-range fighter escorts that made such raids as the Dresden attack tactically feasible. Saundby, as deputy to air Chief Marshall Sir Arthur Harris, leader of RAF Bomber Command, implemented the Dresden raid, albeit "with considerable misgivings."[38] Eaker's account is of the flag-waving variety, but even Saundby's regret is couched in terms that justify the immense destruction of the raid: it remains a caution that the simple banning of nuclear weapons will not make warfare less destructive, for even the most conservative estimates of Dresden's losses exceed Hiroshima's by almost twice, while a conventional raid on Tokyo killed 17 percent more than the greatest atomic attack.

Rumfoord needs these texts because he is filling in a gap in the official history of the United States Air Force, the gap created by the Dresden raid's status as a top secret operation even twenty years after the event. And so his role as the USAF's official historian is the same as Vonnegut's as author and Billy's as a time traveling witness: to fill in this central absence with details surrounding the event. To the texts enveloping the bedridden historian Billy adds one more, his extremely short but potent testimony of witness: "I was there" (165/191). Rumfoord, who despises Billy's weakness, characterizes his status with a text borrowed from Theodore Roosevelt, "I could carve a better man out of a banana" (159/184). He denies Billy's testimony, and resents the fact that he is even allowed to live, crippled as his mind and body appear to be. As for Billy, he continues doing what people without power try to do: "He was trying to prove to a willfully deaf and blind enemy that he was interesting to hear and see" (166/193). Rumfoord remains an intractable listener, and Billy escapes his disapproving presence only through time-travel; that travelling takes him into further juxtaposed episodes from Dresden. But even momentary intrusions of present-day life cannot remain untouched, for when his formerly renegade son visits him in the hospital, the young man is described as a ramrod-straight leader of men from the Green Berets, exhibiting the same good posture and flawless grooming habits an RAF officer had lectured Billy about during his transit camp internment on the way to Dresden. The last conversation with Rumfoord concludes on a note of Tralfamadorian acceptance, but for the film production of *Slaughterhouse-Five* Vonnegut was called upon to add one more line to close the scene: Rumfoord's dismissal of Billy's act of witness with the scornful admonition, "Write your own book!"[39]

That much of Vonnegut's own experience during World War II serves as part of *Slaughterhouse-Five*'s text is made apparent not just by the author's portrayal of his own efforts writing the book in chapters 1 and 10, but by his identification of himself within the central narrative at three key points: when the distraught colonel from Wyoming searches for his troops among the prisoners boarding the POW train (58/67), suffering from diarrhea after the rich feast provided by British prisoners at the transit camp (109/125), and wondering at the fantastic aspect of Dresden as their train approaches that still unbombed city (129/148). The three episodes are part of the action's transition from combat to imprisonment, the journey that takes Billy and his colleagues (one of them the author) to their fateful quarters in Dresden. As such, the journey encompasses the book's major historical events, reaching from the last major land engagement of the war, the Battle of the Bulge, to the final

German city on Air Marshal Harris's list to be bombed, Dresden. Between these two events, Vonnegut's characters encounter several definitions of the experience of war and its destruction. Each has its own claim on historical validity, just as the texts Professor Rumfoord cites form an argument for the bombing while Billy's experience as a character and Vonnegut's as an author make a case against it. Mary O'Hare, after all, had warned Vonnegut not to glamourize his and her husband's adventures, while Billy's fate has been to have his life disordered by a similar inability to speak about what happened in the war. On the way from the Bulge to Dresden, Billy Pilgrim and Kurt Vonnegut hear several explanations for what is going on, each of them a model account. One by one, however, these models are dismissed, emptying the matter of Dresden of presupposed meaning so that the experience can be seen for what it is.

The first interpretation is Roland Weary's. A friendless individual with little to recommend him, Weary is possessed by images: horror stories about mutilation and torture, a pornographic photo of a woman having sexual congress with a pony, and fantasies of comradely support reminiscent of *The Three Musketeers*. He relishes all three, and all three are taken from him, until he becomes one of the action's first casualties. His interpretations, like himself, do not survive. They do, however, provide fuel for another interpretation, that of the rabid little American known as Paul Lazzaro, whose dreams of violent retribution sustain him through the war but lead to his reduction to a killing machine, impelled by his viciousness toward that day in the distant future when he will assassinate Billy Pilgrim for allegedly killing his buddy, Roland Weary. Lazzaro's model fails, however, because it is based on patently untrue assumptions. Billy's stumbling onto Weary's infected foot is scarcely evidence for murder; Weary has never been anyone's buddy; and Weary has died in Edgar Derby's arms, not in Lazzaro's, as Lazzaro would have his listeners believe. His story fails to bear the test of truth, as does the advice of a former hobo among the transported soldiers who insists that he has seen worse riding the rails during the depression. "You think this is bad?" he keeps asking. "This ain't bad" (68/79). This final repetition serves as his dying words.

More controversial is Vonnegut's rejection of the British prisoners' response to war. Thanks to the noble characterization of the British war effort through Winston Churchill's speeches and the gallant fighting of the RAF during the Battle of Britain, Americans have been schooled in the admiration of "the few" who fought to save England during her "finest hours." A long tradition of historical literature, fiction, and film further enhances the British wartime cause, especially the mystique of high discipline and unremitting effort among prisoners of war in Douglas Bader's *Reach for the Sky,* Paul Brickhill's *The Great Escape,* and especially Sir Alec Guinness's role in the film *The Bridge on The River Kwai.* It is a helpful coincidence that thirteen years before *Slaughterhouse-Five* was published, Vonnegut's group of prisoners makes an appearance in one of these British war memoir classics, Geoff Taylor's *Piece of Cake.*[40] An Australian trained in the Royal Australian Air Force and attached to RAF Bomber Command, Taylor flew a Lancaster shot down on a mission to Hanover late in 1943. After eluding his captors for a day, he was interned as a POW for the war's duration, eventually winding up at a camp just north of Dresden. From there Taylor and his fellow internees marked the war's progress by noting how the British and American bombing raids reach farther and farther east, until the sight of B-17 Flying Fortresses at altitude become a common occurrence. "Standing bare-footed in the sun one morning and waiting for your daily issue of turnip you watch a Fort being shot down," Taylor notes during the summer of 1944. As an airman, he knows the American flyers are over 500 miles from their base in England, and that their pursuit by two Focke-Wulf 190s promises to be fatal: "Even by the time you have shuffled to the head of the shambling queue and are chasing the larger lumps of turnip around in the big iron pot with your jam-tin mug, the Fort and the fighters are still crackling at each other in the distance" (144). He and a fellow RAF veteran remark on how the agony is being prolonged, but end their brief conversation with some words about how thin the soup is today. Straining off the water, he asks another comrade, who has been watching, how the B-17 is doing:

"They've had it," comes the reply.
They certainly have. From the window you can see a cloud of

black smoke rolling up into the sky from the distant high ground on
the other side of the Elbe. They didn't get very far.
So it goes on, day after day. (145)

The use of *Slaughterhouse-Five's* same tag line, "So it goes," as a
commentary on the airmen's deaths indicates a common attitude toward the war—an attitude Professor Rumfoord encouraged Billy to
share when asking him to empathize not just with those suffering on
the ground but also with "the men who had to *do* it" (171/198) from
the air, a situation Billy accepts with a Tralfamadorian sense of neces-
sity. The possibility of divergence comes with the ways Taylor and
Vonnegut variously judge the British POW model of conduct. Taylor
portrays the British style in the same terms Vonnegut does, but obviously approves of its method and appraises its success in contrast to
the Americans' shabbiness:

> The British airborne men—paratroopers, glider pilots and glider
> troops [captured since the Normandy invasion and the costly assault at
> Arnhem]—have a bearing and pride in themselves that is good to see.
> They are a walking justification of that overlooked phrase, "esprit de
> corps." If it comes to that, the morale of most of the new British army
> prisoners is good. Oddly enough it seems to have something to do with
> the fact that the British battle-dress with its identifying shoulder
> flashes and insignia is the kind of rig in which a man can go into action,
> fight, be taken prisoner and arrive in the cage still looking much the
> same sort of soldier as he started. What's more, it's serviceable. Much
> of the clothing worn by American troops seems only to look soldierly
> and serviceable when it has come from the cleaners. The British
> troops, too, are noticeably quicker at settling down in the stalag. Al-
> most immediately they are busy scrounging around, organizing them-
> selves and "tin-bashing" old cans into plates and mugs, which is the
> only way of getting such utensils in the stalag. (158)

The great influx of American prisoners comes with the Battle of the
Bulge, an action Taylor's group has learned about from the Nazis' propaganda newspaper and clandestinely monitored BBC broadcasts. "Until
the German drive in the Ardennes is halted," Taylor notes, "the camp is

poisoned with an atmosphere of mean, illogical contempt of the Americans who failed to hold von Rundstedt" (178). The hindsight of military history and Vonnegut's portrayal of Billy Pilgrim is more revealing of the truth: many of the American units crushed by the German offensive were green, untested troops, only recently brought forward to replace the veteran divisions that had landed on 6 June 1944 and fought on for the next six months until the front was supposedly secured through Belgium and Luxembourg. Whether smarter uniforms would have made them tougher fighters and better disciplined prisoners is questionable, but Taylor prefers to focus on his own group's activities: first expressing impatience and annoyance at having to receive thousands of new prisoners in their already overcrowded camp, but then, realizing that the Americans have had a bad time and will be in poor shape when they arrive, settling down to a project of tin-bashing and tidying up so that their welcome will be a hospitable one.

"The first mass of the American prisoners arrives outside the stalag just before the sun goes down in Christmas Eve," Taylor notes, and proceeds to verify historically the scene presented years later in *Slaughterhouse-Five*. The unit described is Kurt Vonnegut's:[41]

Through the western wire you see them, a myriad of dark forms huddled in the snow beneath the distant pines. The Germans leave them out there all night.

Beginning with the next morning, Christmas Day, the days that follow are quite the most depressing you have ever experienced in the stalag. Standing at the main gate you watch a large part of an American infantry division—the 106th—stumble into captivity. Never before have you seen men so near the end of their tether. Plagued with dysentery, twisted with frost-bite, starving, dirty, unshaven, staggering on their feet from exhaustion, a long line of men stumbles endlessly into the camp.

Captured before they knew what hit them, marched hundreds of miles into Germany, stepping over the bodies of comrades who slumped to die in the snow, jolted for days in cattle-trucks and boxcars that were strafed and bombed by the Allied air-fighters, the Americans are macabre burlesques of men.

Sometimes a man staggers and bumps the man next to him and

they snarl weakly at each other. They are too shocked and dazed to do otherwise. The frosted air is alive with the bark of men coughing. A lot of them won't live to walk again. This is the end of the road. Outside the wire, by the Kommandantur office, a mountain of GI battle helmets and liners grows visibly bigger, dwarfing the Germans who stand by it. Inside our barracks, confusion also reaches fantastic heights.

It's just as well we organized the bunks and tin-bashed mugs and plates for the new arrivals. The shambles would have been unimaginable had we not. As it is, our carefully-balanced world of unwritten tabus, tribal laws and customs reels under the impact of thousands of men so shocked by their experiences that many are little more than animals stumbling erect. (179–180)

The correspondences to Vonnegut's internment scenes are uncanny, down to the physical details of Billy Pilgrim stumbling into Roland Weary. Not that Vonnegut drew upon Taylor's memoir, for he was not aware of *Piece of Cake* until I showed it to him in 1987. The point is that verifiable history surrounds Billy's fictional experience within *Slaughterhouse-Five,* and that the contrary British and American models for the prisoners' response to the war are based in fact—on a series of facts so stable that authors recalling them independently, a dozen years later in a war memoir or two dozen years afterward in a novel, manage to report the identical, precise details. Taylor even agrees with Vonnegut's interpretation that for the Americans this war had been a children's crusade, given their relative innocence:

A GI tells you about the German snipers.
  "I saw one of those goddam Krauts," he recalls.
  "Did you shoot him?" you ask.
  "Hell no," says the GI, "he woulda shot back."
  You don't think he's kidding. Five weeks before he saw the German sniper in the pines the GI's only association with the war had been as a clerk in an army equipment depot in New Jersey. He just hadn't had time to get used to the idea of firing bullets at total strangers. (181)

One last detail corroborates Vonnegut's skepticism with the British model; for, as Taylor admits, the cozy and ordered life-style accomplished by the long-term RAF and British Army inmates has been helped along by "an unexpected and miraculous issue of Red Cross food" (181).

Vonnegut and his fictional characters survive the Dresden raid by virtue of their deep underground shelter. Taylor, true to his model, has been struggling to escape, since according to his service's code that is the prisoner of war's first duty. On the night of 13–14 February he finds himself hiding in the woods, having slipped away from a work detail with plans to steal a German aircraft from the nearby Luftwaffe base at Lonnewitz and fly home. Dresden itself is only twenty-five miles away, and from his vantage point in the open Taylor can view the raid in its entirety. But what he sees is pure spectacle, little more than the sea of fire Vonnegut later views in Marcel Ophul's film and the visual equivalent of the ominous sounds Billy Pilgrim hears walking around overhead:

> You crawl out of the foxhole and, walking clear of the pines, try to see what you can see. To the south, beyond where Stalag IVb lies, the sight is almost appalling. The night sky is stark and brilliant with the cloud-reflections of bomb-bursts, fires and photoflashes. It looks and sounds like a thousand thunderstorms run riot. (211)

But as for understanding the fate of Dresden's inhabitants, Taylor can voice no sensations—all he can feel are the "drumming of continuous earth shocks" (211) transmitted to his body. The next day his hiding place is strafed by the same marauding P-51 Mustangs who drove the Dresden fire brigades back into their shelters, but Taylor's thought are understandably for his own welfare, wondering why the Yanks must bring their war to his part of the woods. Like the action of *Slaughterhouse-Five*, Taylor's war ends several weeks later with his guards disappearing, leaving the prisoners to wander about in search of repatriation. Flown back to England, Taylor is greeted by a group captain who shakes his hand and asks if he has had a good trip. Like his fellow author, Kurt Vonnegut, and like Vonnegut's creation, Billy Pilgrim, Taylor finds himself at a loss for all but the simplest and least meaningful words. "Unexpectedly jaunty in a lightheaded sort of way, I was startled to hear my own voice replying, inanely: 'Yes, thank you sir. A piece of cake'" (273).

"Piece of cake" is RAF slang for an easy operation, no trouble at all. Taylor's return from his mission to Hanover has taken over a year and a half, during which time he has suffered much himself and seen the war's scope enlarged to encompass a destruction hardly imaginable on his own last raid in 1943. Yet his ability to articulate the facts of his experience to his first sympathetic listener add up to little more than *Slaughterhouse-Five*'s own summation, the bird call of *"Poo-tee-weet?"*

Where Taylor and Vonnegut diverge is in judging the British prisoners' way of structuring the war. In *Piece of Cake*, their discipline and spirit is seen as a sustaining device, especially in contrast to the Americans' ragtag behavior. In *Slaughterhouse-Five*, Vonnegut portrays his countrymen in scarcely better terms, for their conduct makes them almost as bad as the Nazi propagandist depicts them: as "the most self-pitying, least fraternal, and dirtiest of all prisoners of war" (113/131), despising their own leaders and betraying their comrades for personal gain. Paul Lazzaro is the worst of them, and his own model is discredited; but even the best of them, Edgar Derby, cannot survive, his good-natured spirit and dedication bringing him only to a firing squad's bullets. The Nazi propaganda, which would seem to be discredited by its source, echoes Kilgore Trout's social philosophy espoused at the end of *God Bless You, Mr. Rosewater*, at least when it comes to explaining why common Americans lack a sense of dignity. The British prisoner's style certainly looks better, and has underwritten a long tradition of noble stories. There is no *The Great Escape* produced by Billy's battalion, nor is there a *Bridge on the River Kwai* among their experiences. On the balance, Howard Campbell's assessment claims the better part of truth: *"Expect no brotherly love, even between brothers. There will be no cohesion between the individuals. Each will be a sulky child who often wishes he were dead"* (113/130).

The British prisoners conduct themselves as gentlemen. One of them gives Billy and his comrades a stern, uplifting lecture on the sustaining benefits of good posture and correct personal hygiene. They are generous hosts, and good soldiers, all of them having tried to escape at least once. But Vonnegut is quick to indicate flaws in their model, founded as it is on distortions of the truth. As for their continued dedication to escape, "They could tunnel all they pleased. They would inevitably surface within a rectangle of barbed wire, would find themselves greeted listlessly by dying Russians who spoke no English, who had no food or useful information or escape plans of their own" (80/93). Their dedication to order is underwritten by a clerical error that has sent them five hundred Red Cross parcels for every fifty deserved, none of which they share with the starving Russians. When they do outspend themselves in hosting the incoming American prisoners, it is because of a similar misappraisal: "They were so elated by their own hospitality, and by all the goodies waiting inside, that they did not take a good look at their guests while they sang. And they imagined that they were singing to fellow officers fresh from the fray" (82/95). But the greatest distortion is the falsehood on which their relative well-being is founded: "They were adored by the Germans, who thought they were exactly what Englishmen ought to be. They made war look stylish and reasonable and fun" (81/94).

Because the British prisoners' restructuring fails the formal test of changing reality, Vonnegut dismisses it along with the other models considered previously, including Roland Weary's comic book fantasy of the Three Musketeers and Paul Lazzaro's gangsterlike dream of personal retribution. What warfare is may exceed one's ability to articulate and describe, but from all the evidence presented in both Taylor's and Vonnegut's books it certainly is not stylish and reasonable and fun. The British prisoners have tried to transform war's sordid reality into something more acceptable, but their attempt is simply one of style. Vonnegut's own transformation will be of form, to his mind a far better approach to the matter of otherwise inexorable content.

That transcending the matter of Dresden is no easy undertaking is established by the historical record. The most exquisitely detailed realism in *Slaughterhouse-Five* is devoted to Billy's capture, transportation to Dresden, and experiences in the bombing's aftermath. These passages are powerful testimony not just to war's horror, which is always beyond words, but to its petty and insistent degradation of the individual. Vonnegut incudes himself in this central action thrice; he thereby positions himself as a public writer addressing a great public event. Yet there must be a difference between the war as it appears in a novel and as it stands recorded in the pages of history, if fiction is to have any distinguishing property at all. History books, newspapers, films, and in our own day television can give us the news; but as theorist and novelist Ronald Sukenick cautioned, only fiction can give us our response to the news, and before a final judgment about *Slaughterhouse-Five*'s effectiveness can be made it is helpful to note Vonnegut's own historical record about the war.

That record exists in two letters preserved among his family's papers. The first is dated 29 May 1945—just a few weeks after the repatriation described in *Slaughterhouse-Five*'s closing pages, where Vonnegut has rejoined his fictional characters to close the book's action both in terms of depicting events and finishing the novel. It is signed "Kurt—Jr." and addressed to his father at the family's Williams Creek home in Indianapolis. Its salutation, "Dear people," includes not just his father but his brother, sister, aunts, uncles, and cousins of the Vonnegut clan, all of whom are cast as the first readers of Pfc. K. Vonnegut, Jr.'s (12102964 U. S. Army) first war story, factual as it is:

I'm told that you were probably never informed that I was anything other than "missing in action." Chances are that you also failed to receive any of the letters I wrote from Germany. That leaves me a lot of explaining to do—in precis:

I've been a prisoner of war since December 19, 1944, when our division was cut to ribbons by Hitler's last desperate thrust through Luxemburg and Belgium. Seven Fanatical Panzer Divisions hit us and cut us off from the rest of Hodges's First Army. The other American Divisions on our flanks managed to pull out: We were obliged to stay and fight. Bayonets aren't much good against tanks: Our ammunition, food and medical supplies gave out and our casualties out-numbered those who could still fight—so we gave up. The 106th got a Presidential Citation and some British Decoration from Montgomery for it, I'm told, but I'll be damned if it was worth it. I was one of the few who weren't wounded. For that much thank God.

Well, the supermen marched us, without food, water or sleep to Limberg, a distance of about sixty miles, I think, where we were loaded and locked up, sixty men to each small, unventilated, unheated box car. There were no sanitary accommodations—the floors were covered with fresh cow dung. There wasn't room for all of us to lie down. Half slept while the other half stood. We spent several days, including Christmas, on that Limberg siding.[42] On Christmas eve the Royal Air Force bombed and strafed our unmarked train. They killed about one-hundred-and-fifty of us. We got a little water Christmas Day and moved slowly across Germany to a large P.O.W. Camp in Muhlburg, South of Berlin. We were released from the box cars on New Year's Day. The Germans herded us through scalding delousing showers. Many men died from shock in the showers after ten days of starvation, thirst and exposure. But I didn't.

Under the Geneva Convention, Officers and Non-commissioned Officers are not obliged to work when taken prisoner. I am, as you know, a Private. One-hundred-and-fifty such minor beings were shipped to a Dresden work camp on January 10th. I was their leader by virtue of the little German I spoke. It was our misfortune to have sadistic and fanatical guards. We were refused medical attention and clothing: We were given long hours at extremely hard labor. Our food was two-hundred-and-fifty grams of black bread and one pint of unseasoned potato soup each day. After desperately trying to improve our situation for two months and having been met with bland smiles I told the guards just what I was going to do to them when the Russians came. They beat me up a little. I was fired as group leader. Beatings were very small time:—one boy starved to death and the SS Troops shot two for stealing food.

On about February 14th the Americans came over, followed by the R.A.F. their combined labors killed 250,000 people in twenty-four hours and destroyed all of Dresden—possibly the world's most beautiful city. But not me.

After that we were put to work carrying corpses from Air-Raid shelters; women, children, old men; dead from concussion, fire or suffocation. Civilians cursed us and threw rocks as we carried bodies to huge funeral pyres in the city.

When General Patton took Leipzig we were evacuated on foot to Mellexisdorf on the Saxony Czechoslovakia border. There we remained until the war ended. Our guards deserted us. On that happy day the Russians were intent on mopping up isolated outlaw resistance in our sector. Their planes (P-39's) strafed and bombed us, killing fourteen but not me.

Eight of us stole a team and wagon. We traveled and looted our way through Sudetenland and Saxony for eight days, living like kings.

The Russians are crazy about Americans. The Russians picked us up in Dresden. We rode from there to the American lines at Halle in Lend-Lease Ford trucks. We've since been flown to Le Havre.

I'm writing from a Red Cross Club in the Le Havre P.O.W. Repatriation Camp. I'm being wonderfully fed and entertained. The state-bound ships are jammed, naturally, so I'll have to be patient. I hope to be home in a month. Once home I'll be given twenty-one days recuperation at Atterbury, about $600 back pay and—get this—sixty (60) days furlough!

I've too damned much to say, the rest will have to wait. I can't receive mail here so don't write.

This letter, not brought to Vonnegut's attention until May 1987, corresponds closely to the foggily remembered events the author of *Slaughterhouse-Five* struggles to recall. Even the letter's form anticipates the antiphonal response to death used over twenty years later to structure the novel: not yet "so it goes" every time someone or something dies, but rather the conditioned response of survival—"But I didn't," and the twice-repeated "But not me." He does indeed have "too damned much to say" for a short letter, but as reported in the first chapter of *Slaughterhouse-Five* he does not stop trying. His first personal audience for the Dresden tale is his father, his Uncle Alex, and his sister Alice, who pick him up at Camp Atterbury on 3 July 1945 for the drive back to Indianapolis. In Alex Vonnegut's letter of 4 July 1945 to Ella Stewart Vonnegut, the senior Kurt's first cousin, young Kurt (referred to by his family nickname of "Kay"), is characterized as a spellbinding storyteller with a tale of great substance:

Kay is home. At lunch yesterday noon Kurt told me that Alice had telephoned to him. Kay had called from Camp Atterbury. Would they please call for him at about 3 o'clock; he felt certain that he would be able to get away at that time. I was pleased that Kurt asked me to go with him and Alice to get the boy. It was the first time I had been at Atterbury. What an immense place: barracks, barracks stretching over many square miles and thousands of soldiers and many German Prisoners of War. We went to the Officer's Club No. 1, where Kay had told us to meet him. It was ten minutes after three, but no Kay anywhere in sight. Jute [*sic*] boxes playing and soldiers and Wacks dancing. A busy ice-cream stand with pies and Coca-Cola also available. Alice was nervous. She feared she might vomit. We got Coca-Colas and sat on the front porch. A dozen soldiers sitting around passing the time away. The general atmosphere was boredom.

In the distance we saw a tall lad approaching carrying a big heavy bag. Could it be Kay? Those long legs. It might be; it was. We let Alice go to him. A hug and a kiss. "Now no emotions, please!" Kay pleaded. They both wiped their eyes. A hug from his father. A formal handshake from me. The big bag was picked up and carried to Kurt's Dodge car. Kay opened the back of the car and threw the heavy bag in. He is tall as ever, the same long eye lashes, but O that face! Well browned from the recuperation center at Le Havre and the fifteen day trip across the Atlantic.

"I want to drive the car!" He drove us home. I wish I could have taken down in short hand or better yet, I wish I could have had a dictaphone to record what that lad of twenty-two years, (he'll be 23 in November,—November 11th) told us. He speaks well. He is articulate. And he spoke continuously from Atterbury to Indianapolis. But what did he say! What didn't he say? What hasn't he seen? What hasn't he endured and suffered.

Nothing that I can write here will give an adequate impression of what he [illegible] you he was driving and talking, and it's only some forty odd miles from Atterbury to Louise Adams where Jimbo had been parked for the afternoon. As a result of his experiences after being taken prisoner on that ghastly day when the 106th Division was suddenly and quite unexpectedly overwhelmed he lost forty-five pounds. "I had never been really hungry before. I did not know what it means to be thirsty. To be really hungry is a strange sensation. You go nuts! But you mustn't give up. If you give up,—if you don't care, if you lie down and don't care, your kidneys go bad and you piss blood, and then you can't get up again and you just wilt away."

"What do they say over here about the bombing of Dresden?" Yes, we told him that we knew Dresden had been bombed. He saw Dresden before it all happened in 24 hours, he was in the midst of it,—confined with 150 Prisoners in the Municipal Slaughter House which was not bombed,—"as one guy said, 'Well there were once one hundred and fifty pigs here and now 150 Infantry Prisoners.'" Now you lie down in any part of Dresden and see all over the area that once was that beautiful, beautiful city. Hardly fifty houses standing in the vast area. And don't think it wasn't an outrage to destroy that city. You can't imagine what it means. And who was killed? 250,000 men,—mostly older men, of course,—and all the women and all the children. You can't even describe what it means to be bombed. And think of it the people of Saxony never had any use for Hitler and that whole son of a bitch gang. Hitler came to Dresden only twice. He never got a welcome. And Dresden had practically no air raid shelters. It was assumed that Dresden would not be bombed. Everything is gone. All the Art Galleries,—everything.

"What's that scar behind your ear!" Alice asked. That's where the SS beat me. "With what?" "With a scrub-brush!"

And then the tale about their fellow prisoner who stole a can of beans and was tried and had to sign a document acknowledging that he had committed some heinous crime,—he didn't even know what he was signing,—and he didn't know that on the next morning when four of us were taken out with shovels,—and we didn't know that we would have to dig his grave. And in front of it he was shot,—with his back to the firing squad. (And then the driver of Dodge car burst into tears.) "The sons of bitches, the sons of bitches!"

The Russians! "Believe it or not! I was kissed by a Russian Major! He asked me how we were treated by the Russians. I told him just fine!" "He said they were having quite a bit of trouble with some of their own men who were not aware of the fact that the Americans were fighting on our side!"

You ought to see the hordes of Russians that are now swarming in to Saxony. When the advance troops first came all the Germans were scared pink and hid in cellars. But they came in fine order and they threw loaves of bread to the people and they drove in fine American Len [sic] Lease Cars and they were spic and span. But then after a few days came they [sic] hords of Russians,—talk about your southern American negroes. Jesus! Those Russian masses are terrifying. They looted everything in sight. There's not a herd of cattle left in all Saxony. And do you really know what Vodka is like. Jesus! It's just straight alcohol and they drink it by the tumbler full. Really some scientists ought to investigate how it is possible for men to drink such stuff in such huge quantities. They are men. O Christ it was terrible,—the rapings and everything that went on.

"Believe me! I know what's going to happen in Europe. Now the trouble really starts. The French hate the Americans; the Poles and Russians hate the Germans; the Poles hate the Russians; everybody hates the Germans,—excepting the Americans who are giving the Germans five eggs every week in the territory occupied by American troops. And I am here to say that I've got it *in* for the British. They aren't good sports. You ought to see the negro troops in France. They are going big. But don't tell me that the American negro isn't a good fighter. They are just as brave and good soldiers as any of 'em: American, German or Russian. It's fun to see the negroes gamble with their money: "Yeah! Shot another ten spot. I got lots of beaucoup of money, beaucoup of money. And they shoot it away—all of their beaucoup of money. And what they are doing to the French girls. It's no wonder the French feel so bitter against the Americans.

When we arrived at Louise Adams' house we picked up the baby which Kay had not seen since October 1944. It was in that month that he left home. "Kay," I said, "you'll have to be patient with us civilians. We'll probably say things that are mightily offensive to you because we haven't enough imagination to understand what you have gone through." Kay's response was: "O Hell! I want to be a civilian myself. I'm sick and tired of being in the infantry. I want to get out of the army. Look at me. My arm and leg muscles have all atrophied. But I'll have 76 days of furlough here at home and then I'm off to Florida where I'll be housed in one of the finest hotels in Miami. I've got my pullman reservation right here. And then. . . . well,—then what. Damned if I know. But I want to get out of the army I tell you. I want to get out. I've had enough of it. And I'm God damned sick and tired of the whole damn fool bloody mess! I'm sick of it."

This second installment of Kurt Vonnegut's Dresden story thus fades out into the blankness that characterizes his attempts to write about it in the subsequent years detailed in *Slaughterhouse-Five*'s first chapter. His feeling that he has "had enough of it" sustains itself throughout the novel, in which he declines to depict the bombing as anything except a distantly perceived absence. His letter to his father had been structured with incantatory references to his own survival. Now, with his father joined by his beloved sister and favorite uncle as an audience, he locates the experience within his own physical person—yet still insists on the unimaginability of being bombed—something the inhabitants of North American cities went through a supposedly "world" war without experiencing. For them, the mass bombings of civilian populations might as well have never happened. And so the key event from his war story remains unexpressable to his audience at home.

What can they imagine? Perhaps the killing of a solitary human being. And so the death of the person who, nearly a quarter century later, will be known as Edgar Derby and who steals a teapot instead of a can of beans, is described in the specific detail that otherwise eludes Vonnegut in 1945 and again in 1968 as he writes *Slaughterhouse-Five.* Alex Vonnegut, whose letter is the first recorded critical response to Kurt Vonnegut's Dresden story, indicates that it is at this point that his nephew breaks into tears. Throughout the wartime action of *Slaughterhouse-Five,* Billy Pilgrim cries only when the frigid wind brings involuntary moisture to his eyes. Like the little Lord Jesus in the Christmas carol cited as the novel's epigraph and again in chapter 9 (170/197), his Dresden experience concludes "Away in a Manger" with the comforting words of a former enemy that he sleep peacefully. By writing *Slaughterhouse-Five,* Vonnegut has learned to live with death without denying it. Instead of the voluptuous, cleansing, and therefore effacing tears that would wash away historical truth, he transcends it without denying it by acknowledging the inevitable: so it goes. The one-hundredth statement of these words comes at the end, when Edgar Derby's death is finally described.

As for war itself, the author does not flatter himself that one novel or even fifty-thousand words of protest can end such conflict. But if he admits failure at articulating the unexpressable horror of Dresden, he can at least imagine its opposite. Like the best of Vonnegut's writing, this small bit of imaginative transformation is at once comic and touching, practically improbable but at least technically feasible (given mankind's engineering talent and inventive mind), and as achievable by an average person as hitting the reverse switch on his or her home movie projector or videotape player. The occasion is the viewing of a war movie, an act analogous to the readers' experiences making their way through the pages of *Slaughterhouse-Five.* The action depicted within those pages is not determinedly chronological; instead, the author has selected and ordered those pieces of action for an effect other than the inexorable march of history—climaxing with Billy's understanding of his story rather than with the bombing itself, and presenting in conclusion not Billy's psychological disorder in later years but the leafy, bird-songed regeneration of nature following the war. If history is like a movie, a series of events experienced as a continuous presence but adding up to a final product, why can it not be run backwards rather than always experienced the same way?

This process, drawing on the Tralfamadorian notions of time and illusory free will but expressable in the most commonly familiar way (with technology at the fingertips of anyone with a VCR), yields wonderful results when it becomes a war movie. Vonnegut shows one run backward at the start of chapter 4, early enough for his readers to be taught how flexible the human imagination can be when perfected by art. "American planes, full of holes and wounded men and corpses took off backwards from an airfield in England" (63/74), it begins. As the bombers' mission proceeds, Luftwaffe fighters fly up to join them over France, sucking cannon and machine gun shells from the planes and crewmen. Other bombers arise from crash sites on the ground below, and join the others flying backward over German cities, shrinking the fires below them and pulling them up into steel containers held within their bomb bays. They then fly backward to their bases, where the bombs are removed and shipped back to the United States, "where factories were operating night and day, dismantling the cylinders, separating the dangerous contents into minerals. Touchingly, it was mainly women who did this work." The minerals themselves are "shipped to specialists in remote areas. It was their business to put them into the ground, to hide them cleverly, so they would never hurt anybody ever again" (64/74–75).

Such a rearrangement might seem fatuous in terms of real life and just a technological trick when it comes to artistry. But the effect is undeniable, for in viewing a war film history itself is transcended without denying any of its elements except the illusion of causality. Vonnegut's achievement in *Slaughterhouse-Five,* with its conscientious attention to the writer's art of rearranging the elements of his story until they make sense to him, gives readers the chance to experience the world in fresh new ways, and not be prisoners of any one culture's typical forms of description. It may be, philosophers of Vonnegut's age have argued, that not realizing how arbitrary any one formal description is makes people prisoners of a fate that need not be endured. As such, Vonnegut's approach to the matter of Dresden promises a new freedom in understanding his, and our, world.

# Notes

1. C. D. B. Bryan, "Kurt Vonnegut on Target," *New Republic* 155 (8 October 1966):21–22, 24–26.

2. Robert Scholes, "'Mithridates, He Died Old': Black Humor and Kurt Vonnegut, Jr.," *Hollins Critic* 3, no. 4 (October 1966):1–12; expanded as "Fabulation and Satire," in Scholes, *The Fabulators* (New York: Oxford University Press, 1967), 35–55; reprinted as "Vonnegut's *Cat's Cradle* and *Mother Night*," in Scholes, *Fabulation and Metafiction* (Urbana: University of Illinois Press, 1979), 156–62.

3. Leslie A. Fiedler, "The Divine Stupidity of Kurt Vonnegut," *Esquire* 74, no. 3 (September 1970):195–97, 199–200, 202–4.

4. Granville Hicks, "Literary Horizons," *Saturday Review* 52, no. 13 (29 March 1969):25.

5. Robert Scholes, "A Talk with Kurt Vonnegut, Jr.," conducted 4 October 1966 at the University of Iowa and broadcast on the university's radio station, WSIU. Transcribed by Jerome Klinkowitz and published in *The Vonnegut Statement*, ed. Jerome Klinkowitz and John Somer (New York: Delacorte Press/ Seymour Lawrence, 1973), 90–118.

6. Robert Scholes, Review of *Slaughterhouse-Five*, *New York Times Book Review*, 6 April 1969, 1.

7. C. D. B. Bryan, "Kurt Vonnegut, Head Bokononist," *New York Times Book Review*, 6 April 1969, 2, 25.

8. J. Michael Crichton, "Sci-Fi and Vonnegut," *New Republic* 160, no. 17 (26 April 1969):35.

9. Willis E. McNelly, "Science Fiction: The Modern Mythology," *America* 123 (5 September 1970):125.

10. Peter A. Scholl, "Vonnegut's Attack upon Christendom," *Newsletter of the Conference in Christianity and Literature* 22 (Fall 1972):5.

11. Josephine Hendin, "The Writer as Culture Hero, the Father as Son," *Harper's* 249, no. 1 (July 1974):82–87; expanded in Hendin, *Vulnerable People:*

SLAUGHTERHOUSE-FIVE

*A View of American Fiction Since 1945* (New York: Oxford University Press, 1978), 4, 5, 9, 20, 23, 30–40, 44, 49–51, 213, 217.

12. Thomas L. Hartshorne, "From *Catch-22* to *Slaughterhouse-Five*: The Decline of the Political Novel," *South Atlantic Quarterly* 78 (Winter 1979):17–33.

13. John Somer, "Geodesic Vonnegut: Or, If Buckminster Fuller Wrote Novels," in *The Vonnegut Statement,* ed. Klinkowitz and Somer, 221–54.

14. Jerome Klinkowitz, "The Literary Achievement of Kurt Vonnegut, Jr.," *Modern Fiction Studies* 19 (Spring 1973):57–67; expanded in Klinkowitz, *Literary Disruptions: The Making of a Post-Contemporary American Fiction* (Urbana: University of Illinois Press, 1975), 33–61; see also Klinkowitz, *Kurt Vonnegut* (London: Methuen, 1982), and *The Self-Apparent Word* (Carbondale: Southern Illinois University Press, 1984).

15. Alfred Kazin, "The War Novel from Mailer to Vonnegut," *Saturday Review* 54 no. 6 (6 February 1971):13–15, 36; expanded in Kazin, *Bright Book of Life* (Boston: Little, Brown, 1973), 82–83, 86–90; Clinton S. Burhans, Jr., "Hemingway and Vonnegut: Diminishing Vision in a Dying Age," *Modern Fiction Studies* 21 (Summer 1975):173–91; John Gardner, *On Moral Fiction* (New York: Basic Books, 1978), 87.

16. Ihab Hassan, *Contemporary American Literature, 1945–1972* (New York: Ungar, 1973), 47; *Paracriticisms* (Urbana: University of Illinois Press, 1975), 114.

17. Jerome Klinkowitz, *Literary Subversions: New American Fiction and the Practice of Criticism* (Carbondale: Southern Illinois University Press, 1985), xiii–xlii.

18. Jon Stone, *The Monster at the End of This Book* (New York and Racine, Wis.: Western Publishing/Little Golden Books, 1971). Illustrated by Mike Smollin.

19. *Breakfast of Champions* (New York: Delacorte Press/Seymour Lawrence, 1973).

20. *Bluebeard* (New York: Delacorte Press, 1987).

21. *Palm Sunday* (New York: Delacorte Press/Seymour Lawrence, 1981), 296; Vonnegut's commentary on Céline first appeared as his Introduction published in each of Céline's novels reprinted by Penguin Books (Harmondsworth, England, and New York) in 1975: *Castle to Castle, Rigadoon,* and *North,* xiii–xx.

22. "A Special Message to Subscribers from Kurt Vonnegut," *Slaughterhouse-Five* (Franklin Center, Pa.: Franklin Library, 1978), unpaginated; reprinted as part of "A Nazi City Mourned at Some Profit" in *Palm Sunday,* 300–2.

23. Publisher's blurb from the cover of Kurt Vonnegut, Jr., *Mother Night* (Greenwich, Conn.: Fawcett, 1962).

108

# Notes

24. *Mother Night* (New York: Harper & Row, 1966), v. This edition serves as a basis for all subsequent issuings of *Mother Night,* which even though they may involve reset typography all include the Introduction added in 1966.

25. *Breakfast of Champions,* 209–210.

26. Philip Roth, "Writing American Fiction," in *Reading Myself and Others* (New York: Farrar, Straus & Giroux, 1975), 117. Roth's remarks were first delivered as a speech at Stanford University in 1960 as part of a symposium titled "Writing in America Today," sponsored by *Esquire* magazine; as an essay, it appeared in *Commentary* 31 (March 1961).

27. Ronald Sukenick, "The Death of the Novel," in *The Death of the Novel and Other Stories* (New York: Dial Press, 1969), 41.

28. Tom Wolfe, "Seizing the Power," in *The New Journalism,* ed. Tom Wolfe and E. W. Johnson (New York: Harper & Row, 1973), 23–36. Wolfe's essay first appeared as "Why They Aren't Writing the Great American Novel Anymore" in *Esquire* 78 (December 1972):152–58, 272–80.

29. Ronald Sukenick, "Innovative Fiction/Innovative Criteria," in *In Form* (Carbondale: Southern Illinois University Press, 1985), 241. Sukenick's remarks first appeared as part of a publicity statement distributed with his second novel, *Out* (Chicago: Swallow Press, 1973).

30. *Wampeters, Foma & Granfalloons* (New York: Delacorte Press/ Seymour Lawrence, 1974), xix–xx.

31. *Between Time and Timbuktu* (New York: Delacorte Press/Seymour Lawrence, 1972), xv.

32. *God Bless You, Mr. Rosewater* (New York: Holt, Rinehart & Winston, 1965), 210–11.

33. *Ibid.,* 27.

34. *The New Fiction: Interviews with Innovative American Writers,* ed. Joe David Bellamy (Urbana: University of Illinois Press, 1974), 203–4.

35. Donald Barthelme, "Man's Face: A Novel in Forty Coaxial Chapters," *New Yorker* 40 (30 May 1964):30; "Down the Line with the Annual," *New Yorker* 40 (21 March 1964):34–35; "Views of My Father Weeping," *New Yorker* 45 (6 December 1969):56–60.

36. Richard Brautigan, *Trout Fishing in America* (San Francisco: Four Seasons Foundation, 1967), 66.

37. *Slapstick* (New York: Delacorte Press/Seymour Lawrence, 1976), 1.

38. Allen Andrews, *The Air Marshals* (New York: William Morrow, 1970), 271.

39. "Vonnegut Likes ... ", *Yale Daily News* (16 April 1971):1.

40. Geoff Taylor, *Piece of Cake* (London: Peter Davies, 1956).

41. Letter from Kurt Vonnegut to author, 26 April 1987; reading these

passages for the first time, Vonnegut reports, "It is a perfect fit, so our eyes must have met, and he may very briefly have tried to welcome and comfort me."

42. Vonnegut's letter of 26 April 1987 to author remarks that since he did not keep a diary, his own memory is probably less accurate that Geoff Taylor's recollection of the American prisoners' arrival on Christmas rather than on New Year's Day.

# Bibliography

## Primary Works

*Between Time and Timbuktu.* New York: Delacorte Press/Seymour Lawrence, 1972.

*Bluebeard.* New York: Delacorte Press, 1987.

*Breakfast of Champions.* New York: Delacorte Press/Seymour Lawrence, 1973.

*Canary in a Cat House.* Greenwich, Conn.: Fawcett, 1961.

*Cat's Cradle.* New York: Holt, Rinehart and Winston, 1963.

*Deadeye Dick.* New York: Delacorte Press/Seymour Lawrence, 1982.

*Galápagos.* New York: Delacorte Press/Seymour Lawrence, 1985.

*God Bless You, Mr. Rosewater.* New York: Holt, Rinehart and Winston, 1965.

*Happy Birthday, Wanda June.* New York: Delacorte Press/Seymour Lawrence, 1971.

*Jailbird.* New York: Delacorte Press/Seymour Lawrence, 1979.

*Mother Night.* Greenwich, Conn.: Fawcett, 1962. 2d. ed., with a new introduction, New York: Harper and Row, 1966.

*Palm Sunday.* New York: Delacorte Press/Seymour Lawrence, 1981.

*Player Piano.* New York: Charles Scribner's Sons, 1952.

*The Sirens of Titan.* New York: Dell, 1959.

*Slapstick.* New York: Delacorte Press/Seymour Lawrence, 1976.

*Slaughterhouse-Five.* New York: Delacorte Press/Seymour Lawrence, 1969.

*Sun Moon Star.* New York: Harper & Row, 1980.

*Wampeters, Foma & Granfalloons.* New York: Delacorte Press/Seymour Lawrence, 1974.

*Welcome to the Monkey House.* New York: Delacorte Press/Seymour Lawrence, 1968.

# Secondary Works

## Books

Bellamy, Joe David, ed. *The New Fiction: Interviews with Innovative American Writers*. Urbana: University of Illinois Press, 1974.

Bradbury, Malcolm. *The Modern American Novel*. Oxford and New York: Oxford University Press, 1983.

Gardner, John. *On Moral Fiction*. New York: Basic Books, 1978.

Hassan, Ihab. *Contemporary American Literature*. New York: Ungar, 1974.

———. *Paracriticisms*. Urbana: University of Illinois Press, 1975.

———. *The Postmodern Turn*. Columbus: Ohio State University Press, 1987.

Hendin, Josephine. *Vulnerable People: A View of American Fiction since 1945*. New York: Oxford University Press, 1978.

Karl, Frederick R. *American Fictions 1940–1980*. New York: Harper and Row, 1983.

Kazin, Alfred. *Bright Book of Life*. Boston: Little, Brown, 1973.

Klinkowitz, Jerome. *The American 1960s*. Ames: Iowa State University Press, 1980.

———. *Kurt Vonnegut*. London and New York: Methuen, 1982.

———. *The Life of Fiction*. Urbana: University of Illinois Press, 1977.

———. *Literary Disruptions: The Making of a Post-Contemporary American Fiction*. Urbana: University of Illinois Press, 1975; revised and expanded, 1980.

———. *Literary Subversions: New American Fiction and the Practice of Fiction*. Carbondale: Southern Illinois University Press, 1985.

———. *The Self-Apparent Word: Fiction as Language/Language as Fiction*. Carbondale: Southern Illinois University Press, 1984.

———. *Their Finest Hours: Narratives of the RAF and Luftwaffe in World War II*. Ames: Iowa State University Press, 1989.

———, and Donald L. Lawler, eds. *Vonnegut in America*. New York: Delacorte Press/Seymour Lawrence, 1977.

———, and John Somer, eds. *The Vonnegut Statement*. New York: Delacorte Press/Seymour Lawrence, 1973.

Lodge, David. *The Modes of Modern Writing*. Ithaca, N.Y.: Cornell University Press, 1977.

Lundquist, James. *Kurt Vonnegut*. New York: Ungar, 1976.

Olderman, Raymond. *Beyond the Waste Land: The American Novel in the Nineteen-sixties*. New Haven, Conn.: Yale University Press, 1972.

# Bibliography

Reed, Peter. *Kurt Vonnegut, Jr.* New York: Warner Paperback Library, 1972.

Scholes, Robert. *Fabulation and Satire.* Urbana: University of Illinois Press, 1979.

_____. *The Fabulators.* New York: Oxford University Press, 1967.

Sukenick, Ronald. *In Form: Digressions on the Act of Fiction.* Carbondale: Southern Illinois University Press, 1985.

Tanner, Tony. *City of Words: American Fiction 1950-1970.* New York: Harper and Row, 1971.

## Articles

Berryman, Charles. "After the Fall: Kurt Vonnegut." *Critique* 26 (1985): 96–102.

Bryan, C. D. B. "Kurt Vonnegut, Head Bokononist." *New York Times Book Review,* 6 April 1969, 2, 25.

_____. "Kurt Vonnegut on Target." *New Republic* 155 (8 October 1966):21–22, 24–26.

Burhans, Clinton S., Jr. "Hemingway and Vonnegut: Diminishing Vision in a Dying Age." *Modern Fiction Studies* 21 (1975):173–91.

Crichton, J. Michael. "Sci-Fi and Vonnegut." *New Republic* 160 (26 April 1969):33–35.

Fiedler, Leslie A. "The Divine Stupidity of Kurt Vonnegut." *Esquire* 74 no. 3 (September 1970):195–97, 199–200, 202–4.

Hartshorne, Thomas L. "From *Catch-22* to *Slaughterhouse-Five:* The Decline of the Political Novel." *South Atlantic Quarterly* 78 (1979):17–33.

Hicks, Granville. "Literary Horizons." *Saturday Review* 52, no. 13 (29 March 1969):25.

Hume, Kathryn. "The Heraclitan Cosmos of Kurt Vonnegut." *Papers on Language and Literature* 18 (1982):208–24.

_____. "Kurt Vonnegut and the Myths and Symbols of Meaning." *Texas Studies in Language and Literature* 24 (1982):429–47.

_____. "Vonnegut's Self-Projections: Symbolic Characters and Symbolic Fiction." *Journal of Narrative Technique* 12 (1982):177–90.

Irving, John. "Kurt Vonnegut and His Critics." *New Republic* 181 (22 September 1979):41–49.

Klinkowitz, Jerome. "The Literary Career of Kurt Vonnegut, Jr." *Modern Fiction Studies* 19 (1973):57–67.

McNelly, Willis E. "Science Fiction: The Modern Mythology." *America* 123 (5 September 1970):125–27.

Merrill, Robert, and Peter A. Scholl. "Vonnegut's *Slaughterhouse-Five:* The Requirements of Chaos." *Studies in American Fiction* 6 (1978):65–76.

Scholes, Robert. Review of *Slaughterhouse-Five*. *New York Times Book Review*, 6 April 1969, 1, 23.

Scholl, Peter A. "Vonnegut's Attack upon Christendom." *Newsletter of the Conference in Christianity and Literature* 22 (Fall 1972):5–11.

Schriber, Mary Sue. "Bringing Chaos to Order: The Novel Tradition and Kurt Vonnegut, Jr." *Genre* 10 (1977):283–97.

Uphaus, Robert W. "Expected Meaning in Vonnegut's Dead-End Fiction." *Novel* 8 (1975):164–75.

Wilson, Loree. "Fiction's Wild Wizard." *Iowa Alumni Review* 19 (June 1966):10–12.

# Bibliography

Pieratt, Asa B., Jr., Julie Huffman-klinkowitz, and Jerome Klinkowitz. *Kurt Vonnegut: A Comprehensive Bibliography*. Hamden, Conn.: Shoe String Press/Archon Books, 1987.

# Index

*Adventures of Huckleberry Finn*
  (Twain), 12
Algren, Nelson, xi
Allen, Fred, 2
*America*, 15
*Angels without Wings*
  (Yarmolinsky), xiii
*At Swim-Two-Birds* (O'Brien), 71

Bader, Douglas, 91
Ballard, J. G., 14
Balzac, Honoré de, 59, 62
Barthelme, Donald, 18, 37, 74–75,
  76, 78
Battle of Britain, 91
Battle of the Bulge, x, 2, 74, 89, 90,
  92–93, 98
Benny, Jack, 2
Boston, xi, 29
Brautigan, Richard, 18, 37, 75–76, 78
Brickhill, Paul, 91
*Bridge on the River Kwai, The*, 91, 96
*Brothers Karamazov, The*
  (Dostoyevski), 69
Bryan, C. D. B., 11
Buffalo Symphony, xiii
Burgess, Anthony, xii
Burhans, Clinton S., 18

Campbell, John W., Jr., 21
Cape Cod, x, xii, 30, 39, 63, 84

Carnegie Institute of Technology, ix
*Céline and his Vision* (Ostrovsky),
  37, 39
Céline, Louis-Ferdinand (Louis-
  Ferdinand Auguste Destouches),
  38–39, 58
Charles Scribner's Sons, x
Chicago, x, 28
Churchill, Sir Winston, 91
City University of New York, xii
Clarke, Arthur C., 56
Clement, Hal, 56
*Collier's*, x, xi, 3
Coover, Robert, 49, 71
*Cornell Sun*, ix
Cornell University, ix
*Cosmopolitan*, xii
Cox, Jane, x; *see also* Vonnegut,
  Jane, and Yarmolinsky, Jane
  Vonnegut
Crane, Stephen, 78
Crichton, J. Michael, 14–15

*Death of the Novel and Other
  Stories, The* (Sukenick), 18,
  62–63
*Death on the Installment Plan, The*
  (Céline), 39
Delacorte Press/Seymour Lawrence,
  xii, 75
Dell Publishing Company, xi

*Destruction of Dresden, The* (Irving), 88

Dickens, Charles, 59, 60

Donoso, José, xi

Dos Passos, John, 21

Dostoyevski, Fyodor, 69

*Double or Nothing* (Federman), 18

Douhet, Giulio, 88

Dresden, x, 2-3, 4, 5, 6, 7, 8, 10, 13, 16, 22, 26-27, 28-29, 30, 31, 33, 34, 36, 39, 40, 41, 42-43, 44, 46-47, 48, 49, 57, 63, 64, 73, 77, 81, 82, 83, 84, 86, 88, 89, 90, 91, 95, 97, 99, 101-2, 103, 104, 106

*Dresden, History, Stage, and Gallery* (Endell), 36

Eaker, Ira C., 88

*Eden Express, The* (Mark Vonnegut), xii

Endell, Mary, 36

*Esquire,* xi, 63

*The Exagggerations of Peter Prince* (Katz), 72, 78

*Extraordinary Popular Delusions, and the Madness of Crowds* (Mackay), 36

*Fabulators, The* (Scholes), xii

*Farewell to Arms, A* (Hemingway), 18, 22

Faulkner, William, 21,

Fawcett Publications, xi

Federman, Raymond, 18

Fiedler, Leslie, 11-12

Fielding, Henry, 22

Fitzgerald, F. Scott, 4

Gardner, John, 18

Gass, William H., 78

General Electric Corporation, x, 3, 28

Goethe, Johann Wolfgang von, 36

Great Depression, ix, 1

*Great Escape, The* (Brickhill), 91, 96

Guinness, Sir Alec, 91

*Harper's,* xi, xii

*Harper's Bazaar,* 3

Harris, Sir Arthur, 88, 90

Hartshorne, Thomas L., 17

Harvard University, xii, 88

Hassan, Ihab, 18

Heinlein, Robert, 14, 21, 56

Hemingway, Ernest, 18, 21

Hendin, Josephine, 17

Hicks, Granville, 12-13

Holt, Rinehart & Winston, xi

Indianapolis, ix, 1, 45-46, 98

*In Watermelon Sugar* (Brautigan), 75

Iowa City, 45, 84

Irving, David, 88

*Joseph Andrews* (Fielding), 22

*Journey to the End of the Night* (Céline), 38

Katz, Steve, 37, 49, 72, 78

Kazin, Alfred, 18

Kennedy, John F., xi, 63

Kennedy, Robert, 8-9, 15, 22, 40, 63

King, Martin Luther, 15, 63

Klinkowitz, Jerome, 17-18

Krementz, Jill, xiii

Laurel & Hardy, 2, 87

Lawrence, Seymour, xi, xii, 28-29, 44, 75

*Life,* xi, 63

*McCall's,* 63

McNelly, Willis E., 15-16

Mailer, Norman, 18, 21

*Memory of Justice, The* (Ophul), 42, 44, 95

Mitchell, Billy, 88

# Index

*Monster at the End of This Book,*
    *The* (Stone), 23–25, 26
Morgan, Henry, 2
Müller, Gerhard, 26–27, 28, 33, 34, 35
*Mysterious Stranger, The* (Twain), 12

*Naked and the Dead, The* (Mailer), 18
*New Journalism, The* (Wolfe and
    Johnson), 61
*New Republic,* 14
New York, xii, 61–62
*New Yorker, The,* 74
*New York Times Book Review,* xi

O'Brien, Flann (Brian O'Nolan), 71
O'Hare, Bernard V., 28–29, 30–31,
    33, 34–35, 36, 40, 41
O'Hare, Mary, 30–31, 36, 41, 45,
    51, 70, 72–73, 90
Ophul, Marcel, 42, 44, 95
Ostrovsky, Erika, 37, 38, 39

PEN/American Center, xii
Perelman, S. J., 74, 75
Philadelphia, 28, 30
*Piece of Cake* (Taylor), 91–96

*Random House Dictionary, The,* xi
*Reach for the Sky* (Brickhill), 91
Reagan, Ronald, 63
*Red Badge of Courage, The* (Crane),
    78
*Redbook,* xi, 3
*Rocket Ship Galileo* (Heinlein), 22
Roethke, Theodore, 37, 38, 39
*Rotarian,* 63
Roth, Philip, 59–61
Royal Air Force, x, 46–47, 88, 89,
    91, 95, 96, 99

*Saturday Evening Post,* xi, 3, 11
*Saturday Review,* 12
Saundby, Sir Robert, 88
Schenectady, x, 28

Scholes, Robert, xi, xii, 11, 13–14
Scholl, Peter A., 16–17
"Sesame Street," 23, 26
Shortridge High School, ix
*Snow White* (Barthelme), 18
Somer, John, 17
*Sound and the Fury, The* (Faulkner),
    22
Starr, Harrison, 27
Sukenick, Ronald, 18, 37, 49, 61–63,
    72, 74, 78, 98
Susann, Jacqueline, 66, 67, 69
Swift, Jonathan, 12

Taylor, Geoff, 91–96
Thackeray, William, 62
*Tristram Shandy* (Sterne), 22
Trollope, Anthony, 62
*Trout Fishing in America*
    (Brautigan), 18, 75–76
Truman, Harry, 88
Twain, Mark (Samuel L. Clemens), 12

United States Army, ix–x, 2
United States Army Air Force, x, 29–
    30, 46–47, 88
*Universal Baseball Association, J.
    Henry Waugh, Proprietor, The*
    (Coover), 71–72
University of Chicago, x, xii, 3, 28,
    29, 47, 59
University of Iowa Writers Work-
    shop, xi, 4, 11, 28, 38, 45, 47,
    74, 84
University of Notre Dame, 12
University of Tennessee, ix
*Up* (Sukenick), 72, 78

*Valley of the Dolls* (Susann), 66, 67, 69
*Venture—Travelers World,* xi
Vietnam War, 14, 63, 82
"Views of My Father Weeping"
    (Barthelme), 75
Vonnegut, Alex, 100, 103, 104

Vonnegut, Alice, xi, 100, 101, 102
Vonnegut, Bernard, x
Vonnegut, Edith Lieber, x, 98
Vonnegut, Ella Stewart, 100
Vonnegut, Jane, xi, xiii, 29, 31; see
    also Cox, Jane, and
    Yarmolinsky, Jane Vonnegut
Vonnegut, Kurt
  Biography, ix–xiii, 1-5, 98–103
  Critical reception, 10–18
  Work on *Slaughterhouse-Five*,
    21–106

  WORKS (drama and television)
  *Between Time and Timbuktu*, xii,
    64
  *Happy Birthday, Wanda June*,
    xii, 64

  WORKS (essays)
  *Fates Worse Than Death*, xiii
  *Palm Sunday*, xiii
  *Wampeters, Foma &
    Granfalloons*, xii

  WORKS (fiction)
  *Bluebeard*, xiii, 30
  *Breakfast of Champions*, xii, 30,
    33, 58–59, 70
  *Canary in a Cat House*, xi, xii
  *Cat's Cradle*, xi, xii, 11, 14, 65, 70
  *Deadeye Dick*, xiii
  *Galápagos*, xii, xiii

*God Bless You, Mr. Rosewater*,
    xi, 11, 65, 67–68, 69, 70–71,
    80, 96
"Hal Irwin's Magic Lamp," xii
"Hyannis Port Story, The," xi
*Jailbird*, xiii
"Lovers Anonymous," xi
*Mother Night*, xi–xii, 11, 45, 46–
    47, 48, 65, 81, 85
*Player Piano*, x, xi, 11, 64–65
*Requiem*, xiii, 5
"Report on the Barnhouse Effect," x
*Sirens of Titan, The*, xi, 11, 56,
    65, 70, 79
*Slapstick*, xii, 2, 87
*Slaughterhouse-Five*, xii, 4–5, 6–9,
    10–18, 21–106
*Sun Moon Star*, xiii
*Welcome to the Monkey House*, xii

Vonnegut, Kurt, Sr., ix, 98, 100,
    101, 103
Vonnegut, Mark, xii
"Vonnegut's Attack Upon Christen-
    dom" (Scholl), 16–17

Wall Street, 1
Wolfe, Tom, 61–62
*Words for the Wind* (Roethke), 37, 39

Yarmolinsky, Jane Vonnegut, xiii
Yates, Richard, xi

Zelazny, Roger, 14

# About the Author

Jerome Klinkowitz received his B.A. and M.A. degrees from Marquette University, and his Ph.D. from the University of Wisconsin in 1969 with a dissertation on Nathaniel Hawthorne. His 1972 Dell anthology, *Innovative Fiction,* introduced a radically new group of American writers, whom Klinkowitz examined at length in *Literary Disruptions: The Making of a Post-Contemporary American Fiction* (1975). Since then he has written ten additional books on contemporary fiction and has edited nine others, including (with John Somer) Kurt Vonnegut's first collection of essays, *Wampeters, Foma and Granfalloons* (1974) and (with Asa Pieratt and Julie Huffman-klinkowitz) the definitive bibliography, *Kurt Vonnegut: A Comprehensive Bibliography* (1987).

Professor of English and University Distinguished Scholar at the University of Northern Iowa, where he has taught since 1972, Klinkowitz has also worked as a rock and jazz musician and serves as executive director of the Waterloo (Iowa) Diamonds, a class-A minor-league farm team of the San Diego Padres. His award-winning collection of baseball fiction, *Short Season and Other Stories,* was published in 1988. He is at work on a study of the jazz musician Gerry Mulligan.